C000022815

FORWARD

The following stories are some of what really does happen while serving in Her Majesties forces, some names have been changed to protect those who may otherwise sue me or just do not wish to be named.

From being a civilian to soldier then back to civilian followed by a taste of seventies civilian life and back into uniform again, some people may recognise themselves, some may not want to, others may just not give a damn.

I see some of my ex army colleagues from time to time when we have reunions, some of us keep in touch by Email or even phone calls.

Having read several books on military anecdotes like "Brasso Blanco & Bull" by Tony Thorne, I thought that I would tell some of my amusing experiences and events too, so I hope reader that you enjoy this read.

CHAPTER 1

My family had a military type background, what with Dad having served in the two world wars both in the Royal Horse Artillery.

Horse back as a messenger in first, a motor cyclist messenger in the second, however at the end of the first war the horse he had fell on him smashing his right hip which he got over quite quick from all reports but then in the second world war the motor cycle fell on him smashing his hip yet again, but this time he had complications set in and had to have a pin through his hip which incapacitated him quite a lot so was then invalided out just before the end of the second world war.

My brother George decided to join the Catering corps when it was his time to do his national service, so he signed up and did six years most of them in Hong Kong lucky beggar that was in the late forties and early fifties then my brother John was conscripted and he joined the Beds and Herts. Light Infantry and ended up being posted to Korea during that war, however George being the elder of the two tried getting John posted to Hong Kong with him away from the fighting John took exception to that and told him (brother George) to get stuffed and was able to tell George in person while on R & R leave in Hong Kong.

John served his full term in Korea before being discharged, and from the time he came home to the time he got married he was a quieter man than before his enlistment, we did manage to glean from one of his mates that while he was on his R & R in H K with George his team where ambushed on a routine soiree and all where lost this obviously upset John but he never spoke of it himself.

Then came the time for Brother-in-law Mick to be conscripted and he decided to sign on as a volunteer to get better pay which was a bit hard on those who didn't like the idea of being conscripted and also did not wish to stay in the Army any longer than the two years national service.

It all started at Christmas nineteen sixty when the whole family had a get together for the first time in ages, as a clan that is! Well while we were enjoying the festive season, we had two members of the family who were waiting to go abroad. Sister Mary and her husband Mick were about to embark for a place called Randerath in western Germany, Mick had joined the Army and had been in Germany for about a year and it was now time for Mary to join her Husband. Who had been given a private letting as he called it just out of the town which was a stones throw away from the Camp where he was stationed?

Mick had joined the Royal Artillery but was now seconded to the Army Air Corps as a store man.

As the beer flowed, the more Mick started to run off at the mouth, "you should join up Mike" he said "you would enjoy it at least you would be able to travel and see the world", he said, "yes" said my Dad "why you don't join the cake I don't know" he said, "it will make a man of you at least".

"Go on mate" said brother-in-law George Fossey or "haven't you got the guts"? "Oh! Piss off you prat", I replied. "You cheeky little git, if I get hold of you I'll give you a smack round the mouth", "bollocks" I said, "why don't you mind your own business you fat prat" I said. (George and I didn't like each other).

I turned and started to speak to Mick, who tried to convince me to join up, so I said that I would think about signing up the following week, but, I didn't know what Regiment I should sign up for, so I said that I would wait to see how I do on the entrance exam first. It turned out to be a choice of either the Royal Signals or the Royal Artillery, and I plumped for the Artillery.

I signed on at St Albans Army Recruiting Office, not just to get the Queen's shilling either, I received my instructions and rail ticket to go to a place called Oswestry, "where the hell is that?" I remember saying to my brother. "In Shropshire it says on my draft papers." "Well that's where it is then, you prat!" "OK," I said, "keep your bloody wig on."

The day came for me to report to the train station and go to the training camp, I was instructed to travel by train to a station called Gobowen, where I would alight the train and board a transport which would take me to Park Hall training camp in Oswestry where all recruits would be welcomed to the training regiment.

Nobody shed a tear as I waved goodbye, I think every one was glad to see the back of me, bloody charming, I thought.

After boarding the train at Boxmoor station I met a chap on the train going to the same camp so we settled in a compartment by ourselves and gave each other the answers to each other's questions, what's your name, where do you come from, how did you come to sign on and stuff like that.

I remember thinking before I answered his question as to why I joined, "why did I?" I didn't really know the reason, was it because all my family had been in the forces was it because I had been badgered into it, or was it to get out of the rat race that had become civilian living? I really didn't know, I guess part of me wanted to improve myself, while I was a kid I was always on the side of the winning team of soldiers so maybe it was a natural extension of being a kid fighting imaginary wars, what I didn't know or could have known was how far that extension would stretch.

We came to know quite a lot about each other by the time we heard the stationmaster shouting, "Gobowen, all new recruits for Oswestry out here, all recruits out here." So we jumped off the train with our little bags from home with our washing and shaving kit and change of clothing, not ready for what was about to greet us.

As we left the train we saw that we were not the only ones going to the camp, "Ok" a voice shouted from the end of the platform "come on you lot, get yer arses down this end or you will miss the transport".

As we climbed on the lorry I noticed that all the lads were all the same as my new found friend and I, fresh faced, little knowing what was to come, eyes wide with fear at the unknown. "What's it like?" I heard someone at the front of the lorry say,

"Oh don't worry boyo you will soon get used to it, I did," and then nearly every one on the lorry was trying to ask this Welsh lad a question at the same time.

"You will soon find out boyo's" he said, "just you see if you don't." When we reached the camp we were greeted by what I can only describe as a Bulldog in uniform, he was loud mouthed, foul-mouthed and I don't think he had a father either! "Get down you 'orrible lot," he shouted, we all to a man jumped down and stood shaking in our shoes, all but my new found mate, Johnny. "Come on, come on," shouted the bulldog, "what's your name, you orrible worm?" he shouted at Johnny. "Johnny, mate" said Johnny, "what's yourn." "Get fell in you worm," he shouted at him, "before you feel the toe of my boot, you little git." "Get out of the wrong side of the bed did we?" said Johnny, "shut up" I hissed at him "shut your mouth you big twit, can't you see he is about fit to bust," and with that Johnny fell in beside me, "ok, ok, keep your hair on" he said.

I think that Bulldog heard him and said to us both, I will see you two after you have been introduced to the Regiment, what are your surnames we told him and he made a mental note of them and we walked off, sort of in step, towards some buildings that which we later knew as the stores.

Here we all collected our Army Issue clothing including olive green Boxer shorts Yuk!! And we had to put all our civilian clothes in a case, which would now be kept in a lock up for future times.

Then we were all lead to our billets and Johnny and myself were put into the same billet, which pleased the pair of us. The billet was called a spider six legs leading off a main corridor where the Ablutions where, each leg housed a troop of trainees, which had eight beds down one side; eight beds down the opposite side and two large coal burning round stove type heaters, in the middle.

Each bed had a window over the head and a large locker stood beside each bed and on the opposite side of the bed was a bedside cabinet, the floor was polished wood and made an awful sound with every body walking up and down.

It felt really cold and uninviting; at the windows were some dark blue curtains, very cold I thought very cold indeed.

4

After we had chosen what bed we wanted, we had to go to the Barber, "Christ! Whoever called him a barber must have been either blind or pissed", said Johnny as we waited outside for the rest of our room-mate's to have hair cuts.

"Christ look at my hair", he kept saying "look at it, how am I going to face my bird when I go home with a hair cut like this? Go on you tell me that", he said, "oh for gaud sake, shut up Cheeseman", I said "mine is as bad as yours and every one else is going to be in the same boat, but you don't hear them moaning do you"? After the last hair cut, we were taken back to our billet and told that was it for the day, but we would be getting a visit from our respective NCOs' who, would teach us a few basics.

Like bulling boots, ironing our kit and folding said kit correctly, some of us knew how to bull boots so we started to do just that. After a couple of what seemed hours but was only minutes, a tall skinny NCO came in the room who was a Bombardier (two stripes).

"Tennnn shun", shouted the bombardier, and every one stood up, "what did he say" said Johnny, "oh just get up John for Christ sake just get up", so he did. The door burst open again and the three striper came in the room.

"I am your Troop Sergeant, Sergeant Smith with a Tee Aitch not double F got it", and he was greeted with a couple of yes, yer and ok's, he didn't like our response and let us know that we should answer in the following manner, you will all shout at the top of your voices, "Yes Sarge! Is that clear you horrible bunch of crap", yes sarge we said, "louder" he shouted "I can't hear you".

Yes Sarge! We all shouted, "That's better" he said "now make sure I get the same answer each time right", Yes Sarge! Was the response. "Right girls" he said, "in the morning you will be taken to the M O, for a medical and god help anyone who doesn't pass".

"Then we will be taken to the Battery Office, where we will fill in some paperwork provided your can all write, after that we will take a little stroll, then we will go back to the M I room for some jabs.

You will all now write down your new address so that you can write to your Mothers if you have one, you are now in The 24 Irish Battery, 17th Training Regiment, Royal Artillery, Park Hall Camp, Oswestry, Salop short for Shropshire got it", "yes Sarge"

"It is now time for your tea you all know where the cookhouse is now, so off you go; oh bye the way Gunners Hook and Cheeseman, I have a special request job for you two. Report to the cook sergeant after tea and he will give you an introduction into one of the niceties of Army life".

"That's just great", I said to Johnny as we walked to the cookhouse for tea, "you and your big gob, we only just arrived and already we are in the shite" I said. Oh "stop shinfin" he said "at least we will get some more tea after all the squaddies have finished, yer but we will be too tired to drink it, you prat"! I said.

We had our meal then duly reported to the cook sergeant who told us we had to wash up all the utensils from that meal which included the plates cooking utensils the whole shebang, "John remind me to keep bloody quiet when your around will you", "do give it a rest" he answered.

After washing the whole of the items that are present in the Army kitchen we retired to our room completely knackered.

The following morning we where awakened by a noise that sounded like a crash had occurred in the Billet.

I jumped up in blind panic to see the squad Bombardier, banging on a dustbin lid with his pace stick; "rise and shine" he shouted, "hands off cocks and onto socks, come on rise and shine". This was to be the start of what was to be the rest of my life and for some reason I was looking forward to it, albeit with some foreboding!

We where taught how to hold a rifle while we marched up and down the length of the parade ground. We were also drilled to the peak of performance, we where taught how to read maps and how not to get lost while out in the exercise area for training how to look after ourselves in the great out doors.

We had to go through a rigorous fitness routine daily, in the gymnasium and on the assault course, which we were sure was designed by a sadist and helped by a masochist, just to put a final hardship to the course. We were insulted to distraction daily, by our Troop Sergeant and the Troop Bombardier, just for fun.

We were subjected to early morning calls to allow us to enjoy the early morning bird song, but none of us wanted to listen to the birds at that time in the morning. All we wanted to do was sleep until at least twelve thirty, but we didn't get the chance, not even at the week-ends, as we had to rise at six so that we didn't get used to our beds as the NCO's put it.

The one thing that did change for me was the fact that I had put on some weight and I noticed that I had grown about an inch in height during my training. Of course I had become fitter than I had ever been before; this made me feel good about myself, even if it was hard. I was beginning to enjoy the training, as hard as it was; it was doing me the world of good, just as my father had said before I left home to join the Army.

I remember that after we had been given our Military Number and told that we must remember it so that every time we are asked for our number we would be able to recite it automatically with out thinking. Eight weeks after getting used to 23821142 my number was altered as, another soldier had been given the same number in 59 Aston Battery.

My number became 23821140. Although it was only the last number that was changed this threw my ability to recite the number at will, right out the window for about three days. I kept getting it wrong and after some more spud bashing at the week-ends, I am sure that helped me, as I didn't want to do too much spud bashing, I really didn't!

It was half way through our training, when we where allowed to go home for a long weekend. This meant that we left the barracks on Thursday night and was required to return by six pm, on the Monday evening, and woo betide any one who is late, said the Troop Sergeant. The long week-end seemed to fly, I was soon back in the Barracks and wishing that I was back home, but after a couple of days, I was right back into it again, enjoying the training.

I look back sometimes and ask myself, was I a masochist to enjoy all the pain that I was subjected too while in training, or was I just plain daft? Or was it just that I enjoyed feeling fit for the first time in my life?

It was now the end of the training and the pass-out Parade was to take place the following day and we where all bulling boots, webbing brasses plus applying fresh Blanco to webbing, ironing our uniform or pressing the locker lay-out ready for our final inspection by the Camp Commander, the Colonel.

We chatted to each other hoping that we would all get the posting that we had asked for.

I had asked for Hong-Kong, my second choice was Malaya, my third Germany. Some of the lads wanted to transfer to the Army Air Corps or wanted to go into the PT Corps and some like me just wanted to go abroad and see the world, but we wouldn't find out until after the Pass-out Parade.

The whole of the training Regiment was called on Parade at Eight am, we had inspections by! The Troop Sergeant assisted by the Bombardier, then the Troop Officer followed by the Regimental Sergeant Major.

(The whole Regiment consisted of Eight Troops from each of the two training batteries 59 Aston Battery and 24 The Irish Battery).

After waiting a further half an hour we then had a final inspection by the colonel and his 2 I/C. We then had to march passed the stand with the Colonel, the 2 I/C, and Regimental Sergeant Major.

Our own Battery Commander, as well as the Wives and Girlfriends of the lads on Parade.

We marched for at least an hour, and all of us were ready to drop by the time we were given the order to fall out. This was given after we gave three cheers to ourselves and threw our berets into the air to signify the end of our training. All the lads who had family at the parade went to join them, this left about five of us without family, so we decided to make our way to the NAAFI canteen for a couple of beers.

After we had been in the canteen for about an hour we went back to our billet, on arriving at the hut we saw most of the lads milling round the notice board.

"What's up" I said. "It's orders for our postings," came a voice from within the melee, "oh great where am I going." "Can't see" said Johnny but I've got Malaya. "Jammy sod" I said.

"Come on some body where the bloody hell am I going is it Hong Kong or what?"

"Well it looks like you are going to the same regiment as me." said Geordie. "Where is that then," I said. "A place called Nienburg, West Germany." "Oh bloody hell I wanted H.K." "Well you didn't get it mate, never mind said Johnny, you might get a posting to H.K. after a while with that Regiment."

"No chance," came a voice from the melee "24 have just come back from Malaya, so you don't have a cat in hells chance mate." "Oh bollocks that's just about my luck that is."

"Look at the bright side at least you only have an over night trip on the troop ship we have two bloody weeks." "How about you and me swap your two weeks for my twelve hours," I said.

"You piss off, he said, I will stick with what I have," with that I walked away feeling dejected but not really surprised.

I was told that I might not get what I wanted in the first place, but still it would have been nice to have got Hong Kong first, so I will just have to make the most of it.

That night most of the lads who had to wait for the morning before catching the train home, for a two week leave, had a get together in the NAAFI canteen, with nearly all of them getting drunk, even the troop NCO's joined us for a couple of drinks, which showed us that maybe they did have fathers after all.

We had a sing-a-long and then fell, rolled or crawled back to the billet for the last time. In the morning no body shouted for us to get up and it seemed weird.

No Bombardier banging on the dustbin lid, no Sergeant shouting to get out on parade, it came as a bit of a shock to the system at first but I guessed that we would all get used to it eventually.

We gathered up or kit bags, cases and off we went to the station boarded our individual trains and departed Johnny and I got a compartment by ourselves, as we did when we first met before training, we gave each other our new Regimental addresses and promised to keep in touch. I got out of the train before Johnny, at Hemel so, I bade him farewell and as the train pulled out of the station I felt a lump come to my throat, this is probably the last time I will see Johnny, "bye mate" he shouted "be lucky"! "You too" I replied, "see you, bye"!

I walked away from the station wandering if I would ever see him or any of the lads again.

CHAPTER 2

I spent two weeks at home on holiday, I visited some of my old school mates while I was at home, knowing that it may well be at least two or three years when I would see them again. After that sort of time some of them will have moved, some may be married plus any other eventuality, so I made sure that I saw as much of them as I could before reporting to Woolwich Arsenal, which was at that time, a transit camp for the Artillery, plus the Head Quarters.

I arrived at Woolwich hoping that I would soon be off to Germany. But I was to get a shock and that was, I was to go to Germany at the end of June and I will be travelling on my own as all the other lads would be going over in a week.

I was picked to do some dogs' body work at the Arsenal, all that time, along with other duties. I was either on guard, working in the Sergeants Mess or the Officers Mess, I was really fed up by the time June came around and ready for my troop ship ride so I thought.

The day came when I had to report to Harwich docks to catch the Troop Ship to the Hoek-Van-Holland; I was transported to Harwich by three-ton truck with my Kit Bag, wearing full webbing and Battle Dress, accompanied by several soldiers going back off leave to respective Regiments in Germany.

We reached the docks at nine in the evening I reported to the Transportation Office, which was manned by two humans, (the reason for this being said will become apparent) I was asked if I had any other baggage, "only my kitbag and what I stand up in" I replied.

I was shown to a waiting room, which stood in for a cafe, canteen, and dining room, it was clean the chairs we all had to sit on were hard and uncomfortable, and we all sat in this large room until the Ship was ready to receive us all.

We started to board the ship at Ten pm, we were met by NCOs shouting profanities at each and every one of us, we were all crammed into bunk beds under the main deck each deck had three tiers of bunks; I being naive thought that I would be smart and grab the bottom bunk, this turned out to be a wrong move and a really bad judgement on my part and one that I would regret and never forget.

After all those going to the Hoek were on board we set sail, and as we did a loud cheer went up from nearly every one on board, this was at that time something that happened each time a ship left England for foreign soil.

We had been sailing for about thirty minutes, when off went this deafening siren and NCOs started shouting for every one to get up on deck.

We scrambled up the narrow stairways which no body "apart from the Ships crew" was used too, people started to trip on the stairs and this made the situation worse. As one person tripped it was as if this started a shock wave, as every one seemed to trip.

Of course the stair ways just got crammed with bodies trying to climb over soldiers who had tripped, and all the while the NCOs were screaming and shouting at us, as if we didn't hear them.

"Shut up shouting for Christ sake" said one chap, "I'm pissed of with this" said another, "who's idea is this anyway" said another, "don't ask me I said just get up the stairs before that prat bursts a blood vessel".

We arrived on deck and were all standing to attention as we had the welcome address from the Ships Captain, then another address by the Ships: Adjutant. Who informed us that as we had taken such a long time to parade on deck we would undergo another Fire Drill as he called it, we all called it a pain in the neck! "And other things".

It must have been about two hours after returning to our bunks that I was awakened by a chap above me shouting. "What's going on I asked?" "It's this dirty bastard above me", he said, "he has just puked up over me".

As he said that the lad was trying to get down to the floor and as he passed me he started to throw up and yes you guessed I was the receiver of the whole lot, "you shithouse I said you rotten git, you could have held it", and with that he started to throw up again so I quickly turned him round facing the opposite way and told him, piss off!, as I was making my way to the toilet area so that I could clean up, the bloody siren went.

Oh Christ I muttered and turned round and started for the stairway this time nobody tripped and we all reached the deck without incident.

As I stood on parade a couple of the lads looked me up and down and asked "what the hell happened to you?"

"Oh some prat decided to have a kit check just before the siren went off, and I didn't get chance to clean up."

I stood in line smelling bloody awful, then one of the NCOs notice me talking and he went mad, he shouted that I was a bloody disgrace to my uniform.

As I tried to speak to him to tell him how it happened he was not in the least interested, "you scruffy urchin," he yelled at me.

"You can now get yourself to the galley and report to the cook Sergeant for duty." "But!" I said, and was cut short by the NCO shouting at me to shut up or I would be on a charge as well as doing fatigues, so I shut up and reported to the galley.

The night seemed to fly by as I had to work in the cookhouse yes you guessed, peeling the bloody spuds and washing up the utensils used by the cooks while going about the task of getting breakfast for the crew. At least I was able to clean myself up too. It was about seven a.m. the following morning, when we arrived at the port of Hoek-van-Holland.

As far as I was concerned it was a welcome relief, as this meant that I could leave the rest of the chores to the soldiers going back to blighty, on the return trip.

We were all shepherded into a very large dinning room and given a breakfast meal. Which consisted of shrivelled up streaky bacon, two rashers.

One over cooked sausage, a ladle full of baked-beans and an egg, which looked as if it missed the frying pan altogether. It was a snotty mess and all of this was swimming in grease. Some of the lads just could not bring themselves round to eating any of it some didn't even queue for any food just for a mug of tea.

After every body had been allowed to sit for about fifteen minutes, we were addressed by a very loud Regimental Sergeant Major with an emphasis on the "mental. He was bellowing and shouting, thinking every one was listening to him but I don't thing that any one could hear him over the noise of the Trains that were waiting to take us all to our respective destinations.

As we filed through a gate at one end of the dining room we were asked what Regiment we had been assigned to, as we answered the NCO at the gate told us what colour train to get on, yes all the trains had colours not names or destinations this would make it easier for us we were told so just look for the colour you were given as I passed the gate "Nienburg I shouted", "Yellow train" shouted back the NCO.

Off I trekked to the yellow train; I reached the train and boarded as I did so did a couple of lads who were Engineers, "where you going sprog"? said one of the engineers to me, "oh Nienburg" I said, "change at Monchengladbach" said his mate, "ok, thanks" I said, "its quite a long trip, so if I was you I would get your head down for a sleep we will give you a shout" offered the thin Engineer, "ok thanks", I said again and started to make myself as comfortable as possible.

I must have slept for ages because when I woke I was being shaken by a German train guard, "come on! Come on! English! Come on" he said "wake up you must get out here this is the border", "Border? What bloody Border?" I said. "Brunsweg" he said. "Berlin, come on out you get." As I alighted it dawned on me that I had been taken for a ride in more ways than one.

I was confronted by a very mean looking Military Policeman who said in a low grunt. "Where are you supposed to be maggot?" "Nienburg" I said. "Oh and why the fuck are you at the Berlin station?" he shouted a little louder than he needed too. "I don't know"

I said, "Well lets see he said, if I was you I would get back on this train when it pulls out again and return to Hanover where you will get off and then board the green train to Nienburg do you understand maggot?" "Yes corporal" I said, with this the NCO turned purple, "Corporal! Corporal! He stuttered Staff you little maggot he shouted even louder, Staff, do you hear me?" "Yes Staff" I said and ran along the platform just in time to jump on the train which was returning to Hanover.

As I settled in the compartment on my own with just my kitbag as company, I thought back to the two engineers who must have had a good laugh at my expense. Bastards I thought, I hoped that I see them again so that I am able to do them a favour, bastards I thought again.

I managed to reach my destination without any further problems, and reported to the Regimental Guardroom.

"You the new bloke? Just got in have you"? said the Gunner at the Guard house door, "yes" I said, "ok mate, he said just come with me and I will show you which Battery your in," so I followed him to a large building, that was behind the Guard room and at the other side of the Parade ground, which we marched round not across, as this was hallowed ground, if a Soldier was found on the Parade ground when not taking part in a Parade or March practise he would be scrubbing said Parade ground with a tooth brush, I kid you not.

I was shown where to go for my bedding, where the Mess Hall was and the NAAFI told who to report to the following morning and informed that the Regiment was out on Exercise for the next week and that I would be working in the Cook House, shit I thought not again. It wasn't long before the Regiment came back off training and I was introduced to all and sundry, like the Garage area where all the Vehicles would need to be washed and cleaned and painted as we were being visited by one of the Royal Family later in the year.

You have never seen so much bullshit in all your life, if it moved you saluted it, if it didn't move you painted it, if it was silvery you buffed it, if it looked like silver you painted it to look even more like silver, and of course this was only July the visit was not until November, so why all the bull now? I asked a senior soldier, we have got UEI prior to the Royal visit he said then we have Admin week then we have a two week training camp at Bisbingen on the ranges, as well as border patrol (this was pre the Berlin Wall) I wish that I hadn't asked now!

We washed and cleaned, we polished, we painted any thing and every thing, by the time we had finished we had to wear sunglasses so we didn't get eyestrain or flash back.

Being new to all of this, I asked several soldiers what were all the different inspections for. It turned out, that this was normal, every year was the same, you had Regimental Inspections but before that you had Battery inspections and if you where really lucky you even got a Troop inspection first.

Then came the UEI this stands for Unit Equipment Inspection, this was always followed by the Admin Inspection which some times took the guise of an inspection by the Brigadier and his Aide-de-camp who was a colonel, oh and of course we also had the NSI Nuclear Sureity Inspection by the American Forces, due to having yank equipment at the time.

But, in between times you can go to the NAAFI and have a beer in the evening or go to the Battery bar and get beer, this was the best option as you could fall out of the bar into bed.

It wasn't long before I was one of the lads, none of the lads that I was in training with had been posted to this Battery so I had a whole new start, which I thought that I had made the best of, I shared a room with three other lads and we all had to do our share of the room duties like buffing the wooden floor with a great big polishing mop called a bumper and it weighed in at about fifteen pounds and polished the floor in double quick time.

We still had to ensure that our lockers had the same lay out as in training and the boots had to be bulled each night even our work boots.

Unfortunately I was only allowed out in my Uniform, as I had not been in the Regiment six months and until that time I was not able to wear my civilian clothes outside the barrack gates, but I was still able to go to town and drink in the local Beirhoffs, and Bier Stuber's, unt der Bier Kellar, but we where not allowed to get drunk, if we ever ran into a patrol vehicle from camp we had to hide or we would be taken back to the Barracks and charged with bringing the British Army into Disrepute.

After being at Nienburg for what seemed an absolute age but was only a couple of months, I was asked by one of the Lance Bombardiers if I would assist him with the cub scouts.

I thought well, I can't go out to the town in civilian clothes yet, I didn't like going to town in uniform so I agreed to help out.

We held the cub meetings in a small hut at the rear of the Garage area, which doubled as a Brownies hut on other nights and also a model makers club at weekends.

The first night that I attended the cubs I was given the name of Barghera, by the leader Akalar, reason for the name was that I was quite a fast runner at that time and was now part of the Regimental running team, hence the name of Barghera, as the Panther.

After about three weeks we had the chance of a weekend away from the camp with the cubs, at a place not far from the camp but far enough away to make a difference to our surroundings.

The weekend camp was on the side of the River Veser in a large field where the River flows into a large inlet. This was used for training the cubs for swimming, canoeing and fishing.

We took them for runs in the morning's only short runs, and in the evenings the whole troop would sit round a fire and sing songs, it was really nice.

It made you feel that you were able to give a little bit to the cubs for them to enjoy themselves, and to show them that life is for enjoyment, as well as learning.

After we got back from that week end the Lance Bombardier was posted to England and the troop was disbanded as we didn't have another Rover scout in the Regiment to enable us to carry on.

This led to a bit of a boring time, as I was still unable to go into town in Civilian Clothes.

A couple of month later all the lads from the Battery were looking forward to the Christmas holidays, some had the pleasure of looking forward to going home for the holidays but most of us had just the camp to look towards.

Each room in each Battery began to decorate with streamers and each Battery bar was festooned in all manner of trappings. Plus of cause we had an unofficial Regimental competition to see who had the best decorated Bar, 51 Battery came second this was the Battery that I belonged too, full title was 51 (1841 Kabul) Missile Battery, 24 missile Regiment. (The title was given the Battery when it first served in Afghanistan in that year)

Just before Christmas I woke one morning and as I tried to stand up from my bed I fell over. "What the bloody hell are you doing? said my mate Andy, are you drunk still." he said, I was dazed and was unable to answer him I couldn't feel my right leg or my right arm my mouth was slanted to one side and as I started to answer all I could do was slur my words, I began to panic but it did no good as I couldn't do anything. I tried to stand up again but just fell back to the floor.

I could feel tears welling up in my eye's what the hell is wrong I kept asking myself, I was worried that I might have had a heart attack or something, shit what the hell is wrong I repeated to myself over and over again.

While I was trying to work out what the problem was, Andy had managed to get a stretcher from the MI room and a couple of orderlies.

He burst into the room shouting at every one to move out the way, so that he and the orderlies could get to me and lift me onto the stretcher, I was taken to the MI room where I waited for the MO to see me, as soon as he saw me his instruction was for me to be taken to Hanover Military Hospital. No examination, nothing, just get him to the BMH, so off I went.

On arrival at the Hospital I was greeted by a small Sister, who was very strict, very neat and tidy and very sharp.

"What's wrong with you?" she said, as I was wheeled into the ward, I tried to say "I don't know" but it wouldn't come out and she looked at me and said, "ah! Bells palsy if I'm not mistaken," she said, "What's that?" I tried saying, "don't worry young man she said we will soon have you back in shape," and off she went.

Two or three hours passed before I was visited again, this time by a nurse, she was Irish and her name was Rita.

She told me that I wasn't to worry that all would be ok and that tomorrow the Doctor would explain all, but in the mean time I was to have a bath and an Injection followed by a course of Antibiotics.

After having a bath, which, was embarrassing for me as this was the first time that I had been bathed by a woman since my mother had bathed me when I was a child.

Yes you guessed it was Rita who assisted me with my bath, she never gave the situation another thought she took it, as you would expect from a nurse. Not a flinch from Nurse Rita Finch, god that's bad!

Any way as I was saying after the bath I was treated to an evening meal, and it was a lot better than the meals from the Regimental Mess Hall, the potatoes where cooked the Cabbage was cooked the meat was tasty and well done not chewy or stringy.

It was an altogether better meal, but the only problem was that I couldn't enjoy it.

I had this problem with my mouth, that was it wouldn't do, as I wanted it too, as I tried to chew each mouth full it would escape, out the side of my mouth and dribble down my right cheek onto my chin and back onto the plate.

It must have taken me longer to eat that meal than I can remember a meal ever taking me to eat before or since.

I was like this two months before it started to improve I became adept at eating without making a mess, after spending most of my time sat, in front of a mirror so that I could practice moving those muscles that didn't want to move,

I could see improvement, but it was slow, and having been told that it could last for three months, three years or even life, I was getting a bit worried when after three months; I was still not able to speak without a wobbly gob, as we used to call it.

Then after week one of the third month we could see a marked difference this made me relax and of cause the improvement showed even more.

I came out of the Hospital, and on my return to the Regiment, I was informed that my troop had been picked to do some border patrols, with live ammo, this was scary but it was still at a time when people were trying to escape East Berlin by running through the minefields and through the rows and rows of dannet wire (Barbed wire) soon after that the Regiment was posted to a place called Paderborne.

This is a town south of Hanover, I, on this occasion was rather lucky, as most of the work had been done and to be picked for the advance party would be a bonus for some reason

Well I was about to find out why, as I had been picked to go on the advance party to Paderborne. We left the Regimental grounds at Six thirty am and made our way towards Paderborne, I was in the fourth truck as a co-driver, after we had been travelling for at least three hours we pulled into a rest area on the Autobahn just south of Hanover.

Every soldier got out of the trucks and either went into the café for a coffee or to use the Toilets, we stretched for about twenty minutes then we proceeded to Paderborne.

We arrived at the new camp at about three thirty PM and we looked at the new camp as we drove through the gates.

I remember thinking, oh well, it must be as good as the last camp and at least I will be able to go into town in Civilian clothes, I was looking forward to that more than anything else. The first job was to unload the stores, which each truck had been loaded with; Halfway through the unloading we were dismissed for an evening meal.

As we walked to the canteen we all wandered what type of meal we would get, as we entered the dinning hall we were met by the Provost Sergeant who was the NCO in charge of the advance party.

Good evening gentlemen, enjoy the meal, as you will need all the energy you can get, we have a lot of work for you lucky lads before the Regiment gets here in two weeks time.

True to his word we had lots of work to do after the meal, which was cooked by our own cooks, who came down earlier than the advance group, hence the reason for no comment on the meal.

We started to unload stores into respective Battery stores, Each Battery had its own advance party Des our stores NCO was also our Battery Bar NCO and the first question some of the lads asked was, when is the Bar going to be open Des? As soon as we get all the beer unloaded from the number five truck he said.

I am sure that this gave every man a bit more energy, as we had truck five unloaded before we went to our bunks that night with the added advantage of a beer, from the Battery Bar for free.

All the lads of the advanced party for the whole Regiment joined us we had a sing along and just chatted in groups all but Ginge, he sat at the bar all the time just downing the drinks.

As the evening passed a new lad who sat next to Ginge at the bar, asked Ginge if he would keep an eye on his beer while he went to the toilet, "ok" said Ginge, and with that the new lad left the room.

On his return he picked up his drink and started to drink, when he suddenly noticed that he had something in his drink, it suddenly dawned on him what it was, he just dropped the beer, and panicked, "Christ! what was that?" He asked, with that Ginge bent down and picked up his glass eye and replaced it in his socket.

"You dirty git" he shouted at Ginge. "You asked me to keep an eye on your beer and that is what I did;" everyone in the room was rolling about laughing at the spectacle, all but the new lad that is. The following morning we didn't have a parade as we all expected we just got an early morning call and went to breakfast then given tasks to carry out for the rest of the day.

Unfortunately we still had Guard duties to perform and these came round a lot more regularly than normal, as there were so few of us at the camp. One of the better reasons for not being on the advance party said one NCO, "you should not have volunteered" he said, "I didn't" I said.

"You did" he said. He was right of cause; I had volunteered for nine years hadn't I.

We seemed to be at Paderborne for ages before the main party came to join us, but it was only two weeks. In that time we had achieved quite a lot, we had cleared all the garage area's ready for our own Vehicles to be parked, we had ensured that all rooms, had beds, lockers and any other furniture that we were able to get our hands on.

Most days we worked until nine in the evenings so that we could get weekends off for drinking bouts and going to the local dances at the Bierstube at Sennelager, commonly known as the Barhnhof.

The Regiment came down in three groups over a period of seven days 51 Battery came down with REME.

Then the real work started it took the whole Regiment about a further three weeks to get every thing round to the way that the Commanding Officer wanted the, RSM strutted round the Regiment like a proud Peacock, for the whole of the time. The BSMs of each Battery did their own strutting, upsetting all and changing what was wanted by the BC. Then the Troop Sergeant would come round and change the orders again, so you can see that we got a bit confused at times.

Like all good NCOs, our Troop Bombardiers sorted it all out and the work was always finished on time, but not before a few fucks had been thrown. a couple of the senior NCOs had been called a few choice names and none of these were what their parents had christened them.

We had the choice of doing courses for the furtherance of our careers, and I chose to do a signal's course. We started the course five weeks after our arrival at the camp; I managed to pass the course with flying colours which surprised me somewhat as I found it quite hard to grasp at first.

The worst part was the Morse code; it seemed that every time I received a message it was sent by somebody speaking a different language than me. For a dot, I would think it was a dash, or visa versa, but by the end of the course I managed to make some sort of sense out of it, only to find out that Morse code was being abandoned as a means of communications and only voice was to be used, due to the C13 radios being fazed out as the C45 was preferred. I remember one day being out in the Champ and passing messages to and fro when we decided to have a bit of fun with the Vehicle so we started to drive the Champ in reverse.

Each of us took turns to see how fast we dared to drive backward, as the Austin Champ had five forward gears and five reverse gears this made it quite a unique vehicle to drive.

I managed to get the speed up to forty two miles an hour but I was beaten by Ken Chandler who managed to get up to forty five after playing around for some time we stopped for dinner which was a packed lunch as it was called.

The lunch consisted of Four sandwiches a bar of Chocolate with either an Orange or an Apple

we all had a can of drink or a bottle, as we sat talking Andy and I decided to go to the Barnhof on the following Saturday night to see if we could chat up the barmaid. Saturday came round and it was time for us to get into town, so that we could catch the tram to Sennelager.

We just missed the first tram, and we ran all the way to the tram terminus, Andy said we might as well go and get a drink at the local, as we entered we were greeted by none other than the Barmaid from the Barhnof. Hello Brigitte, hello Mike, are you not going to the Barhn tonight?

Yes as soon as we can get a tram, we both said at the same time. Oh that's ok why don't you come with me, I have booked a taxi, said Brigitte, ok we said so instead of having a drink we all climbed into the taxi Andy in the front seat and Brigitte and I in the back.

When we arrived Andy paid for the taxi and we entered the Bahrnhof, Brigitte went to the Bar to work and Andy and I went to the Dance floor and then to the Bar.

Because Andy had paid for the Taxi Brigitte paid for the first beer. The evening passed quite slowly, but before the end of the evening Brigitte was allowed to leave the Bar as most Customers had either gone or had enough beer so she was not required to work.

All three of us sat at a table listening to the records being played by the DJ and tried to sing along with them, Andy was less able than anybody in the whole of the pub, but still he tried. I could just about manage a few lines of each song, but I do not think that Brigitte was too impressed by our situation at all.

"Why are you two so tipsy." she said, to this I answered, "your fault." "Why, my fault." "If you hadn't given us free drinks all night we wouldn't be pissed said Andy." "Well that's gratitude for you" she said, "hold on a minute Brigitte I didn't say that it was your fault, can I take you home." I said. "What, in your state, you must be joking."

"Ok I said you go then we will walk back to town."

"God I wish I would keep my big mouth shut." Yes you guessed we walked back to town, it's only four miles I said to Andy as we started to walk.

"You idiot Mike why did you say we would walk." "Bravado." "Dick-head said Andy, you really piss me off sometimes and this is one of those times."

"The trouble with you is you have no sense of adventure." "Bollocks he said you must be off your head you really are mad, every time we go out for a drink and a quiet night we end up either walking home or getting pissed and missing the last tram."

"What are you going on about?" "Last time we went out we ended up in the Sennelager nick" he said. "That's only because you forgot to tell me what time it was." "You've got a watch haven't you?" "So, what's that got to do with it?" "Oh, can't you tell the time now then," Andy said. "Piss off" I said, "get knotted," and we walked home the rest of the way in silence.

The following morning we woke and Andy was still very annoyed that we had walked from the pub to the camp, "oh for god sake stop going on about it, I said at least you enjoyed yourself."

"Who said? I did, I didn't, I didn't get a leg over did I." "Well neither did I you prat." "I tried to chat up Brigitte" he said. "You have about as much chance of getting off with her, as I do with the Virgin Mary." I said.

"Well you can't blame a bloke for trying" said Andy, and with that he went off to get his breakfast.

Several Months passed with nothing much happening apart from the mundane things that soldiers do like Parades, Bulling boots, Guard duties, more Bulling boots, Cleaning the Vehicles that were already clean, some more Parades and so on.

I recall one exercise that we under took as being one of all work and no play, in that we were out for six day's and five nights.

All through the exercise we had to move after being set up for a couple of hours, the reason for this was that the type of exercise that we were on was an enemy controlled exercise.

We were on the retreat for the first three day's then we would make a big push and return fire and start the advance, through out the exercise we had guard duties and radio shifts to do.

Unfortunately we had very few extra soldiers to enable us to take turns at having some rest time, so yours truly didn't get any sleep through out the whole of the exercise.

At the time I was driver of a one ton Austin and on the return trip to camp; I was accompanied by, a new. Young Officer, with his dog. The Officers name was lieutenant Entwhistle although a can not recall the dogs name I remember him being a large German shepherd.

On the return trip I was beginning to feel rather sleepy and I said to Mr Entwhistle that I was drowsy, ok he replied at the next pull in we will change round, meaning that we would get some one else to drive while I had a rest.

After about half an hour down the road I must have closed my eye's because as I opened them Entwhistle was trying to pull the steering wheel from my clasp.

"What the fuck are you doing?" I asked, with this he just released the wheel and as he did I saw an old lady on a bicycle disappear under the front of the vehicle, I stopped and got out and the old lady was standing by the side of the road holding her knee and looking rather mad at what had just taken place.

"I am sorry I said and do not have any excuses, other than I didn't see you." With that she just kept saying, "my bike oh! My bike."

Then the German Politzie turned up, took over from my broken German and told us that it would be sorted out, that we would be notified by the local Police what the out come would be, but at the most we would have to pay for the bike and the hospital treatment for the lady.

I was then replaced as the driver and told to get some sleep so I climbed into the back of the Vehicle and slept on the camouflage net.

When we reached the Barracks I was instructed to report to the B.S.M. on doing this, I was told that I was to be charged with, reckless driving, falling asleep while on duty and causing actual bodily harm to a national.

The day of the hearing came and I was called to the Office, as I entered I saw that Lieutenant Entwhistle was already there. "Ok Hook, you are charged with Reckless driving, falling asleep at the wheel of a military vehicle and causing actual bodily harm," do you understand the charges said the BC.

"Yes sir" I replied he then gave me a lecture on letting the British Army down by my actions, and then he said "do you have any thing to say for yourself."

"Yes sir" and I told him about the amount of sleep that I had while out on exercise for the whole duration.

He looked at me in astonishment while I was explaining that we did not have the soldiers we required to fulfil all the duties for the exercise, he looked at Entwhistle who was shuffling uncomfortably and asked "is this correct Mr Entwhistle?" "Yes sir I am afraid it is."

With that the B.C asked the BSM why this had not been investigated further, he replied by saying that Mr Entwhistle had bought the charge in the first place, the BC then gave me permission to dismiss and I left the room with the B.S.M.

As we closed the door of the office the B.C. let fly at the Y.O. he gave him a real royal dressing down.

He was ordered to pay the whole of the fine, which was to have been mine, but in view of the fact that I was not to blame; the B.C. had no alternative but to order Entwhistle to pay instead. I returned to the vehicle-park and just carried on with my duties, all the lads asked what had happened.

I told them and all of them said it served the twit right, he should have known better, and from then on I kept as far away from Mr Entwhistle as I could for a while.

But I needn't have worried, one day we were on duty together and he spoke to me and said that he hadn't realised the effect it had on me and was sorry that it had taken place but that we should now put it behind us, so we did.

I remember just after the whole of the regiment arrived in Paderborne, I was asked by Bombardier Des Goldsworthy, if I would baby sit for him, and I greed to, well you don't turn down twenty marks for babysitting when you're broke, do you?

I arrived at the Bombardiers house at the appointed time to be welcomed by a portly lady who was the Bombardiers wife.

"Come in" she said, I walked in to the sound of the Bombardier shouting down from his bathroom. "Mike! The woman who let you in is Maureen my misses, oh and while we are off camp, my name is Des." "Ok" I shouted back. "Do you want a cup of coffee mike?" Maureen asked.

"Yes please." "How many sugars?" "Two please."

"Both boys are asleep in bed, said Des so you shouldn't have any problems from them." After showing me where everything was kept both Des and Maureen left saying, "we will not be late" and off they went. I read most of the evening, when the parents returned I had fallen asleep on the settee.

"Wake up, said Maureen; I need you to give me a hand with him he is pissed again." "Again! I thought that Des could hold his beer, he always does in the battery bar." I said. "Yes, he can normally, as long as he sticks to beer.

But tonight he thought he would be a show off and drink whisky, and he can't hold it, and this is the state he gets into, I've tried telling him but he is as stubborn as a mule, so now I've given up trying."

We carried Des to the bedroom and I left Maureen to undress him, I went down stairs and made us both a coffee.

After Des was safely tucked up in bed Maureen came down.

We chatted for a while and I was given the life story of the family, being a quiet person I listened intently to her and nodded in the right places.

I left and returned to camp at about twelve thirty, thinking to my self, good god I hope I don't get many more of that type of evening, I really didn't mind the baby sitting, it was the events after the parents return that I didn't care for, still, twenty marks are not to be sneezed at, and Maureen was a lovely Lady.

After a week or so we, that is the Battery went up north to Hohne Ranges for a two weeks live firing exercise, this meant that the Battery was going to fire the Honest John Missile for real.

This was the first time that I had seen a live firing, as all the exercise's to date had been practise only. I was by this time the Battery

Captains Driver and radio operator and as such I would be flitting from range to range to the different Launcher sites.

Major Fawcett was his name and he was known as the B.K. which is the position of Battery Captain the reason for the initials is the Battery Commander, who was Major Smith was given the initials B.C. clear as mud.

We had just driven from one site to the next to ensure that the correct procedure was being carried out, when the B.K. said, "Oh by the way Hook isn't it time for you to renew your drivers permit?" "Err! Sorry sir what do you mean." "The permit for driving, you dim wit!"

"Err! I don't have one" I said. "What? You must have, you are not allowed to drive without one."

"Never been given one" I said. "Don't be absurd he said, every driver has to have one you get it after your test." Pause, "eh! You did have a test Hook didn't you?"

"Err, no sir." "What do you mean no sir, you must have or you wouldn't be driving this Champ, so, how the hell are you?"

"Well, I said, when we were lined up on the advance party from Nienburg, the BSM (Battery Sergeant Major) asked if I could drive, I just said yes and when we reached Paderborne I was then informed by him that I would be driving A one ton vehicle, then you asked for a driver operator and I volunteered and was given this Vehicle." "Right, said the BK I will look into this situation."

And with that we drove in complete silence until we reached the Battery Command Post, the hub of the exercise.

After he had satisfied himself that all was right at this site he ushered me to one side and said, "We are going to the Toc-H for a paper and while we are at it I am going to conduct a driving test, if you fail you will be walking back to Paderborne, have you got that?" "Yes sir," I replied, not wishing to upset him any more than he already was.

Off we drove on the test, after we returned to the CP the BK sat in the Champ and said "OK, you have now passed your test.

You will take this slip to the BSM when we return to Barracks and collect your driving permit and don't forget or you will be charged, is that clear?" "Yes sir, clear as a bell sir." "Don't push your luck, Hook," he replied.

Thank God I passed, the walk back to barracks would have just about done me in, it was at least two hundred and thirty miles back to Paderborne and I didn't relish a walk at all.

After we returned to barracks from the exercise I had the pleasure of explaining to the BSM that I had to have a new driving permit issued, as I was ordered by the BK to do.

The BSM looked at me long and hard then without a blink of an eye, he said. "Where is your old one then Hook?" "Erm, I can't find it sir." "Well why not." "I don't know sir." "You are bloody useless Hook." "Yes sir," I said.

"Get out of this office and don't lose that one." Pointing to the new permit I was holding tightly in my hand. "Yes sir, no sir" I turned on my heels and marched smartly from the office grinning to myself as I left.

That night as we sat in the Battery bar quietly getting tipsy, I replied to one of the lads, who asked me what I was doing in the BSM's office, "Getting my new driving permit." "What, already, it's not due yet." "Ah well." I said, and then proceeded to tell him the tale of the driving permit from start to finish.

"You lucky bastard," he said," I was charged for not having my permit with me on exercise once, how the hell did you do it?" "Luck" I said "just plain luck."

One weekend we had been on a bender to the Bierstube and a couple of the lads had let off steam in town, but had been arrested by the local Police for making a disturbance and being drunk.

All three of them were charged under section 69 of the Army act, which covers every eventuality, in particular being under the influence of drink and bringing the British Forces into disrepute.

This cost all three of them two weeks wages and CB (Confined to Barracks) for a whole month. The one thing that annoyed us all was, the same night; four young officers who had visited the Royal Hussars just up the road from our Regiment had also been apprehended and bought back to the camp.

The only punishment that was meted out to these hapless chaps was a slap on the wrist and don't do it again, reason given for the leniency was that with the young Officers it was high spirits, not hooliganism.

28

I think every man in the Regiment was incensed at the harshness of the sentence for the squaddies and the leniency of the so-called sentence of the YO's.

But of course this was the way the Army was, so we had to accept the rules regardless of if you agreed with them or not.

This also brings to mind another occasion of high spirits, performed by officers of the Regiment.

I remember that it was a Friday due to the Officers mess being superstitious, in that if the thirteenth of any month fell on a Friday this was an excuse for a party and it was called a Black Friday party.

This was one such Friday, I think it may have been about August, or even September, I remember it still being fairly warm in the evenings.

What happened at these nights was that all the Officers in the Regiment would have a best dress dinner followed by plenty of booze.

This particular evening, three YO's got steaming drunk and decided that the Adjutant was an arsehole.

So all three of them broke into his locked room and placed a thunder flash under his wash basin, this promptly blew it off the wall and made a great big hole in the wall were the basin used to be.

However this did not, as you would think, bring the party to a halt, on the contrary, the party just got rowdier, and then it was the turn of the Ac/Adjutant* who himself was a Young Officer.

Unfortunately for him he was a lot less able to hold his drink than the others, so he was carried in his bed to the roof of the mess kitchen. This was a flat roof type, single story building with access to three sides, where upon he and his bed were placed with his large standard lamp at the foot of his bed, his bedside cabinet placed at one side and his car the other side.

Yes, his car! This was a small Fiat, really small, and it took only the three of them to manhandle the car onto the roof….. with the aid of a REME crane.

The only funny part of this episode is that the Ac/ Adj, was still in bed when the rest of the Regiment had been up and about for at least half an hour.

Of cause the news that some one was sleeping on top of the Officers mess roof soon circulated the lads and every one within the camp wanted to have a look., the regiment was laughing about the incident for weeks, but yet again the YO's only got a couple of extra duties each and a slap on the wrist for being high spirited.

Had this been the other Ranks we would have been dealt a very harsh sentence but then again we wouldn't do that sort of thing, would we?

The only time that I can remember a young officer being in hot water, was due to my having the accident in a one ton Austin vehicle when returning from an exercise with Mr Entwhistle and his dog, which was a great big black and tan Alsatian.

As I was driving back to camp both the officer and his dog fell to sleep and both of them started to snore. I remember saying to myself, jees this is all I need I am feeling really knackered and these two are sleeping like babies.

I would like to add at this point that the YO had managed to get sleep each and every night that we were out on exercise. This made me really mad to think that he could just take it easy while I took the sound of him and his bloody dog snoring. That could have put paid to any furtherance of my career.

Not long after that, I was asked if I would like to be the BC's batman, "sorry sir I don't play cricket."

"Not that type of batman you twit," said the troop sergeant. "Oh I see you mean wait on him hand and foot." "No you prat," he then told me what it entailed.

After agreeing a fairly respectful recompense for the work that was required, I agreed to be the BC's batman.

Not long after becoming the said batman I was patting myself on the back, it turned out that for the duties that I had to carry out for the Major I also got out of some guard duties and such like.

Weekend fatigues were a thing of the past, no more spud bashing, no more vehicle cleaning other than the Champ I had to drive.

The icing on the cake was that when I was required to Baby sit the BC's children I got to have a home cooked meal, cooked by the house maid/children's Nanny named Ingrid, who was also head cook and bottle washer and lived in.

One day as I was ironing the Major's uniform, I overheard the Nanny and the Major's wife having a discussion about, Royal Families of Europe.

"What do you, say, Mike." Came a shout from the lounge, "About what mam" I replied. "The royal family, of England."

"I know that we don't have an all English Royal Family in that the Windsor's are originally from the house of Hanover." "Yes, yes, but that doesn't mean that our Royal Family are German, now does it?"

"Well, no not really, but it is still a Bastard throne as it is made up of Greeks and Hanoverians and not English," said the maid.

"Err, could you leave me out of this discussion?

I proffered, I think that it's a little too intense for me and anyway I have a lot to do."

"Cowered!" Said Mrs Smith, "I do not like getting into a difference of opinion with ladies; you sort it out and tell me later." I said and carried on with my work.

The following day the Major came to me as I worked in the garage area servicing our Austin Champ and said.

"I hear you wheedled your way out of a tricky situation yesterday Hook." "Yes sir, the Royal Family is a minefield if you don't mind me saying so." "I quite agree old chap the Major replied. I quite agree, a very wise move on your part if you ask me, he said, good man, carry on." As he strolled off.

"What was that all about?" Came an inquisitive drone from the rear of the garages. "Oh just something that happened yesterday at his house." "Cor! Has he still got that Swedish bird called Ingrid?" said Andy, the voice from the rear of the garage. "Yes."

"You lucky git I wish I could get my end away with her," he said. "Don't be silly she would eat you for dinner." "Yes but what a way to go," he said swooning like a pup.

Time past and it was time for the first winter N.A.T.O, exercise so off we travelled up the autobahn to an area known as Bisbingen cross roads This was an area to the north of the Hohne Ranges that was rather bleak at the best of times and in winter it was bloody awful, winter had just started and we had only had a flurry of snow up to this time but it was icy cold and the wind was biting, every one of us was issued with large coats called a Parka with Liners these where an essential part of daily uniform so that one didn't freeze to death.

The cookhouse was at the front of each Battery's own area lines which was a purpose made field kitchen within old corrugated tin huts, we were provided with a canteen tent for meals and drinks in the evening set up next to the field kitchen, one for each Battery.

After we had erected our tents and all in nice military precise spacing, the vehicles were parked up in each units own lines at the rear of the tent area.

Each tent was issued with an oil stove for warmth and six soldiers to a tent. After being at the camp for about two day's the weather changed for the worst and every one was expecting to return to camp as each day the snow came down heavier than the day before.

But we were ordered by our C.O. to stay put, and stay put, we did.

As I said this was supposed to have been a N.A.T.O. exercise, but the German army returned to Barracks, so did the Danish soldiers, the American soldiers returned to barracks as it was too cold and even the Canadian forces left us.

Not long after that the Dutch soldiers left us saying that we must be mad.

Well, it wasn't us that was mad, it was the C.O. he had decided that we British were made of sterner stuff than the rest, so we stayed put.

We woke one morning and the snow was half way up the side of the tents, and freezing, we made our way to the Vehicle lines only to be met with half the vehicles frozen solid, we couldn't start the engines at all.

Each vehicles crew had too ensure that the vehicle was kept as clear as possible and covered with a large tarpaulin.

This done, we had the rest of the week off other than making sure that all vehicles were serviceable and running ready to start exercise plus we had to take part in sport to keep us occupied.

In the evenings some of the lads went to the beer tents some stayed in their own tents with the heaters turned up to the maximum just to keep warm.

It was on one of these evenings when I decided that I would spend some time in the beer tent so of I went, as I neared the tent I could hear that quite a few of the lads had the same idea.

As I entered the tent I noticed that Ginge and Des were well oiled. "I suppose you two have been at it all day." I said. "No we aint said Ginge just from dinner time innit Des." "Nah for that." said Des in a slurred voice, "can I have an Amstel then Des?" I asked. "No, none left mate." he said, "what! you run out of beer already?" I asked, "no, just Amstel." "What have you got then?" "Hereforder or Dortmunder nothing else," said Des. "Ok I will take a Dab then please." Dab standing for Dortmunder Acton Brewery.

I had a few beers then returned to my tent feeling rather cold, I took off my trousers and jacket but kept the rest of my clothes on, just as every one did, but I still didn't get warm.

I think, in all the time that we spent out on this exercise I didn't get warm very often. I have never been so cold in my entire life.

We had been under canvas now for about four weeks and a slight change in the weather made it a bit more bearable, but not a lot.

Then the weather changed over a period of three days, the days got warmer and the snow started to melt, and the wind dropped at night so this made the evenings slightly more bearable.

On the Fifth week all the snow had melted and every part of the camp area was like a mud pool.

All the soldiers kit in the tents got wet, so we had to hang everything out to dry each day, lads were reporting sick with colds, flue, Diarrhoea and all manner of ailments, but still we soldiered on, because the Colonel said we must.

The exercise went down as the biggest most single cock up of the Regiment at that time and I know that most of us that took part will never forget it for a long time to come.

I ask you, who can forget scooping mud out of boots and sleeping bags then washing all you clothes and hanging them on a makeshift line in the morning and finding them on the floor in the mud at night? You can bet your life that we won't.

Not a lot happened from that point soldiers came and went on different postings round the globe and I just stayed in Germany.

I became sport crazy and took part in as much sport as possible; I joined the athletics team and the Boxing team.

For the Athletics team I ran third, in the Division sports in the four and eight hundred metres and helped the Team come second two years on the trot in the Eight hundred relays.

I only managed fourth in the Four hundred sprint the second year so I gave up running on the track and became a member of the orienteering team. As a team, we managed third place then second place and for two further years we took second place.

During this phase I was also into Boxing I managed to withstand a barrage of punches in my first fight to win on points.

Then I started to box for the Battery and the inter Battery sports was due, I was boxing at lightweight, actual weight was eight stone eight.

Some of the other boxers would try to get into the Gymnasium while we were training but we would send them packing as soon as we discovered them.

The night of the first matches soon came round and I was one of the lucky ones, I got to fight first.

Up I climbed into the ring sat on my stool and waited to be ushered forward by the referee, he called us up, I stood toe to toe with my opponent and just leered at him eye to eye, each trying to psyche the other out, both trying not to show that it was getting to us.

First round we hit each other with every thing that we had, toe to toe, bam, bam, woosh, as a punch flew passed my right ear woosh another, the end of the round came and we returned to our corners.

As I went to sit down the second forgot to put my seat in the corner and yes you guessed I sat flat on my bottom in the corner.

I was really cheesed off at this and the whole of the Regiment had a laugh at my expense, this just made me real mad.

Ding! The second round and I ran to the centre of the ring and waited for my opponent as he walked towards me I let fly with a straight right jab to his middle then a left hook to his head.

He went down like a ton of bricks had hit him on the head, eight, nine, ten, the count was over and I was the winner.

You lucky sod said his corner man, that was lucky punch, piss off! I said and after the ref had raised my hand as the winner I climbed out of the ring.

We watched the rest of the fights and up to that point our Battery had four boxers in the next round, the next round was two days away so we had chance to train some more as well as rest.

The next round started and I was third on the card to box we lost our first man on points although I was the third to box I was only our second man.

I climbed into the ring once more, and as I looked up I saw my adversary who didn't look too good, he was pale and quite thin looking but I knew him as being quite strong, he was one of the NAAFI arm wrestlers, so he was no fool.

The bell sounded and we both started to dance round each other just jabbing out and trying each other, to see who would back off.

To my surprise he backed off, I just followed and as I did I threw punch after punch, he parried most of them but I still managed to get through with some so I was scoring points all the time, but I was getting very little reply from him.

The second round was much the same but in the third round he came at me like a bull in a china shop he just rushed straight towards me but I stepped to my right and he ran passed like a bullet.

He turned stared at me and rushed me again this time I just stood and held out me right fist. Whack he ran straight into it and went down and didn't get up, I looked down at him and he looked up at me and winked but he was counted out so again I was the winner.

After the fight was over and we both climbed out of the ring I went over to him and asked him what he was up to.

"Nothing mate, but I don't want to be in the boxing team, so I thought I would just lay down, beside that, you bloody hurt when you punch and I ain't no bloody masochist.

Good luck in the next round he said I hope you win." I said cheers, shook his hand and went back to the team.

My next and final fight in this competition was to be in three days so I had to prepare for that and under the guidance of our trainer Terry who was the ex Far East Light weight Champion, we started an intense set of training periods. On the day of the finals we all gathered in the Gym and sat in our respective team groups and watched the early matches.

We were also entertained by some of the current BAOR "British Army of the Rhine" champions in exhibition bouts, and then it was the turn of the Battery boxer's.

My match was the first, I climbed into the ring and as I looked at the other corner I noticed that my opponent was wearing a plaster cast on his left arm.

The referee came over to my corner and said, you have got a walk over young man and all you do to win is walk across the ring to his corner, ok? Yes I said and when my name was called I just walked to the opposite corner shook my, should be opponents hand and walked back to my corner, I was then pronounced the winner by way of a walkover due to my opponent not being able to defend himself through injury.

I was the Regimental Lightweight boxing Champ and proud of it too.

Later on that week it transpired that my, should have been opponent, had been out drinking and fell over in the bar breaking his wrist. I went on to fight for the Regiment and won several fights and lost some too but became Light Weight champ.

It wasn't long after that I had to give up boxing due to dodgy eyes, so I took up football and weight lifting as a pass time. Not long after that I was posted, I was sent to the Artillery training school at Larkhill, Wiltshire.

CHAPTER 3

The section I joined was the Missile section under a Captain, called Tommy Laing, who was brilliant.

What he didn't know about Missiles wasn't worth knowing, he was also a disciplinarian, strict but fair, and did not suffer fools lightly, the section always went for a beer after a demonstration to visitors of our capability in the event of action.

I remember one Thursday I was summoned to his office and he said, "Hook what, do you think of promotion, would you ever like to be promoted?

"Well yes sir of cause, but I am on this ERE posting and I am told that the chances of getting promoted under those circumstances are virtually impossible;" "I see said Tommy, just thought I would ask." And with that he dismissed me.

This puzzled me for a while and even spoke to old Dibble about it, we both agreed that it was a strange question to be asked of anyone and I didn't give it any other thought at all.

How ever, all soldiers regardless of rank are supposed to read regimental standing orders especially part one orders as these inform everyone what is happening throughout the establishment.

Like all good soldiers I used to ask someone if they had read Regimental orders over the weekend as I hadn't.

"Yes" said Lance Bombardier Dibble. "Anything on part ones that are of importance," I asked. "No" said Dibble. "That's good," as we walked to our parade, I stood next to Dibble as usual and as Tommy inspected us he stopped in front of me and started to splutter.

What on earth is wrong I thought he looks as if he is going to have a heart attack, me being me asked, "are you alright sir?" "Alright, alright, yes I am but your not you reject, he shouted." I was even more puzzled by his outburst, what on earth is up I thought. "I suggest that you get to a copy of Regimental orders young man he spluttered and when you are properly dressed report to me, in my office, is that clear?" "Yes sir." I replied and ran off to have a look at orders.

To my amazement I had been mentioned in orders and had been promoted to Lance Bombardier, oh shit I thought, no wonder he was upset.

I rushed to the Regimental store and was issued with an armband with one stripe and told by the store man to return with my uniform jackets so that the stripes could be sewn on.

I then returned to the section and waited outside the office for Tommy to return as he passed me to go into his office he said come in bomb Hook and I duly obeyed.

"Right, now young man, why didn't you read orders over the weekend?" "Well I asked someone else if anything was on orders sir and was told that there wasn't sir."

"One word of advice young man and that is trust to no body, for if you do you will sooner or later get into trouble, and today bears that theory out does it not." "Yes sir." I replied, "Right now get out there and be an NCO, I have put my trust in you to carry out your duties to the full, don't let me or yourself down again is that understood Bombadier?" "Yes sir." "Now piss off out of my sight until tonight, I want to see you at the Wagon and Horses, your, buying."

I found out that it was part of being in the section as a NCO; you got to drink with Capt Tom, on occasions.

That evening we sat in the Lounge bar of the pub and we chatted about all sorts of things from Missiles to Rifles, from lorry's to Land rovers and from the church to politics.

Tommy also told me how it was that I had been promoted. I was able to be promoted as I was to be posted to a different Regiment and would not be returning to 51 Battery 24 Regiment. Instead I was to be posted to a different battery and Regiment which could be anywhere in the world, I thought to my self maybe I will get to go to Hong Kong.

I remember we went to north Wales on an exercise for the purpose of firing the H.J. into the sea from a place called Aberporthe just north of Temby, to trial some Radar equipment, while we were there we were billeted in Wooden huts six to a hut, I remember one Saturday the lads didn't have much to do and we were all twiddling our thumbs, when one lad asks. "Anyone up for a séance." A couple of quizzical looks and some eyebrow lifting. "Come on, he said it will be a good, you all keep telling me it's mumbo jumbo so let me prove to you it isn't." All of us agreed so we locked the doors and pulled all the curtains closed, I ensured that the windows where locked too.

Only a couple of lights were switched on so the room stayed quite dim. We all sat round a coffee table which was, by coincidence round, Our colleague from Bristol, Staf had cut some pieces of paper and marked them with signs and happened to have a glass tumbler in his kit, he set the paper round the edge of the table and placed the tumbler upside down in the centre, he ran through what we should do and at no time should any one laugh or speak as this would frighten the spirits away he said.

Well we all placed an index finger lightly on the up turned tumbler as we did Staf said, is any body there? Nothing happened again he repeated the same words still nothing. Someone is not concentrating he said, so we tried again, only this time the tumbler moved slightly. "Piss off said one lad you're moving the glass, you prat." "No I am not, I promise, he said honest!"

So we tried again this time we let the tumbler move and it stopped at each letter spelling out Y.E.S. so he asked "is it Fred and Ada." We had been told before hand the name of his so called spirits, just as well really, as we would have fallen about laughing again, if he hadn't.

"We have some non believers in the room can you let them know that you are present." Y.E.S. the tumbler spelt out, suddenly every curtain in the room blew out and was horizontal as though the wind was blowing them.

Every one except Staf sped away from the table lights were turned up full and the curtains opened. I know that the windows could not be opened and that no way could wind come through them so you tell me how that happened, none of us ever did anything like that again even though Staf tried his hardest to get us to change our minds we all refused, do not play with things that you don't understand was my motto from then on, it wasn't long after this exercise that I was posted to my new Regiment.

At least I would be out of Missiles I was getting a bit fed up with Missiles, so I needed the change that I was about to get.

The date of my posting was creeping up fast and Tommy said that he would be sorry to see me go as we shared some good and bad times.

We understood each other, but as he said, promotion was the name of the game and I had reached the only rank that I could, while at Larkhill so I needed to move on to better myself, needless to say that this was a reason for a party, yes a leaving party.

CHAPTER 4

On my arrival at 27 Regiment I reported to the Regimental Office and the first person I bumped into was a chap I had met on the Troop ship when I first went to Germany.

"Dave isn't it?" I said. "Yes, he said, who are you do I know you?" I explained where we had met and we then chatted about where how why and so on. "You are going into 23 Battery he said, not a bad set of lads as it happens you will soon fit in."

After my induction into the Regiment by the RSM the 2i/c and my new battery sergeant major, I was shown round the Regimental lines.

It wasn't long before I was assigned to a troop and given my duties.

"What qualifications have you got Bombardier," the BSM asked. "I'm a standard two driver operator, sir and I am also a missile number one." I replied. "Well that's no good to you here is it?" He said. "No sir."

"Have you done any gunnery?" "Only with 25 pounders at Larkhill sir and that was only a couple of shoots."

"That's no good either. Jesus, why the hell do we get people, then have to train them up?"

"Sorry sir." "Not your fault Bomb, don't worry about it we will just have to get you trained up that's all, I'm going to put you forward for a standard one driver's course then I want you to go on an O.P. Acks course run by our own NCOs but in the mean time you can be assigned to the Vehicle pool" he said.

(I don't know sir I have never thought about it." "What's to think about? He said, you will go on the next OP course and it starts next month. I want you trained as soon as we get to Lippstadt, is that clear Bombardier?" "Yes sir."

I did my training for Observation Post Officers Assistant and passed, I also enjoyed the course one of the better courses that I took while in the forces as I recall. I did my driver upgrade course and passed as a standard one driver this was really good as it would eventually help me to get promoted again later in my Army career.

After a couple of months some of the Battery Members were picked to go to Northern Ireland on a NATO exercise I was lucky to be picked as the team leader with Johnny Potts as the Land Rover driver with at that time with Gunner Paddy McNare as the Radio Operator.

We were to be the OP Party of a visiting officer from the Indian Army and were introduced to him, his name was Singh and he was a Major who had been trained at Sandhurst Military Academy but his English was barely understandable when he became excited.

As he had once read a book about a Raj soldier who happened to be a colonel with a name close to mine he insisted in calling me Bombadier Hooker.

We travelled over to Ireland by landing craft and the sea was nice and calm until about midnight when things started to get a little choppy, however we landed at the Harland and Wolf dock in Belfast where we alighted our salubrious craft to join the exercise which was held up for four weeks as the Prime Minister at the time One Mr Harold Wilson decided that he would commandeer HMS Fearless, which had aboard the contingent of Marines and Paratroopers that were to take part in the exercise

We waited for the four weeks in Ireland for the exercise to start all this time we were driving round the northern Irish country side practising our role for the coming battle exercise, one morning I remember Paddy cooking breakfast of eggs bacon and beans and passing a plate of this to Major Singh, he went mental he throw the plate down jumped up and down called everyone infidels and stormed off, Paddy looked at me and said "what was that! About?" "Well, I said, I do not think that the Major eats Bacon." "Why the bloody hell not, it was cooked," said Paddy. "I know mate, but I think it might have something to do with his religion." "Oh shit he said I suppose I better apologise when comes back." To which he did and we were all forgiven and then told no more bacon as it comes from an unclean animal.

On one of the weekend breaks we decided to go skating at a town called Newcastle, no not county Durham, this is northern Ireland just north of the Mourn Mountains, I hadn't skated before but both Paddy and Johnny had, so off we went me in the middle of the other two until I was able to stand and skate on my own albeit slowly but on my own non the less.

I was minding my own business and trying to keep out the way of some lads that were all in a line from the middle of the rink to a couple of spaces short of the edge, these guys were going round faster and faster suddenly I fell, down I went with a bump and one of the lads ran right over my out stretched hand. "Shit I said that hurt." "Get up you poof said paddy your alright." "Shit to this I said I'm getting out." I sat in the café until the other two were tired out and came to join me, I bought coffee all round but Johnny wanted a sandwich so he ordered a cheese and jam sandwich with no butter, the girl behind the counter didn't believe him as she had never heard of such a disgusting sandwich before as she put it.

Lucky for me I had only a hair line fracture of the back of my hand so crepe bandage was applied and off I went.

We returned to England and Devises and the Major sang our praises to the BC and BSM who were impressed and actually congratulated us all on a job well done.

After being back in Devises for about a month, the regiment was sent to Cyprus for a tour of duty just as Archbishop Makarius was causing a little bit of trouble, which was partly political and partly religious.

We were there to help to strengthen the forces that were already stationed on the island; these were the UN forces, although we didn't see much in the way of trouble, we still had to show our presence in and around the island as much as possible.

We were based in a small place called Dekelia in between Larnaka and Famagusta on the coast, with the billets facing and next to the sea.

We had manoeuvres in the Truodos Mountains and the surrounding areas. We had just started such an exercise and were travelling up the mountain road, when a local grape carrying truck was careering down the road towards us at a great rate of speed. It was all we could do to get out of the way, we thought that he had lost his braking capacity, but it turned out that this was the normal way for the locals to drive.

As he sped down the mountain the grape lorry was swaying from right to left and was almost on two wheels when he got to the bends in the road. The grape juice was spilling out all over the road and this made the road very slippery, you do not need me to tell you what we thought at that time, I am sure.

You can also imagine the look on some of the faces of the young soldiers, fright, fear, terror, panic, you name it, we saw it on the young faces, and in some cases on old faces too.

That bit of excitement over, we proceeded to our exercise HQ, which, was on the side of the Troudos just by the side of the sea, but we were at the top of a rather steep Cliff face so we didn't get any chance for a swim.

After we had spent the rest of the day patrolling the Melon vine fields we returned to our HQ and had a couple of beers in the mess tent.

While we sat drinking our beers one lad who was nicknamed Marrow, due to every one thinking that he was a bit of a Gypsy and had this awful habit of eating almost anything that walked, crawled or otherwise.

Walked into the tent completely unconcerned and dropped a scorpion onto the table that most of us were sitting at.

The table and the mess tent was cleared in no more than two seconds, the bodies just jumped from the table so fast that all that was left was a cloud of dust.

Graham and I returned, rather gingerly to the tent to see Marrow, sat at the table drinking what was left of the beers that hadn't been tipped over in the rush to vacate the tent.

"You bastard Marrow! We both shouted, what the?" Both stopping in mid sentence, He replied! "It's only a scorpion it won't hurt you, you big girls." He shouted back at us.

"Where is it now." I asked, "Oh I don't know it may be on the floor somewhere."

"Well find the bloody thing and get rid of it, you prat." said Graham, "piss off, Marrow retorted its only a little harmless one anyway." "Just find it and get rid of it." Graham said again. "Oh alright."

When he had ensured us that he had got rid of it we returned to the tent for a last drink, telling Marrow to get out and stay out, which he did.

As I was the duty NCO that night I was the one who had to ensure that the mess tent was closed at ten thirty.

I walked to my Bivouac and started to get undressed and as I slid into my sleeping bag, I felt that the bag was warmer than it should be and for some reason it felt slippery. All of a sudden it dawned on me that I was not alone in this sleeping bag and I shot out of the bag quicker than I got in.

I immediately shouted out "Marrow! You B****** get you arse over here." no answer, "Marrow!" I shouted again.

"Now what's up." he said sheepishly as he came trotting up to my tent. "You know what's up you little git." "I don't know what you are going on about." He replied.

"What have you put in my sleeping bag you shit house." "Nuffink bomb Hook honest."

Well that was like trying to get the pope to have a pint of beer and a leg over, for Marrow to say honest, so I knew that he was lying. "Get what ever it is out of that bag."

"It was only a joke." he muttered as he lifted the bag and shook out about thirty lizards.

"Make sure all of them are out." When I had satisfied myself that all was ok I told him to report to me the following morning.

The following morning at about five, Marrow was pounding on the side of my tent and shouting, Wakey! Wakey! You wanted to see me this morning he shouted, ok! Ok! I replied and climbed from the tent got dressed and started towards the cookhouse tent to make sure that the cook was up and breakfast was on the go, it was.

I instructed Marrow to help the cook until five thirty then to start waking the rest of the Battery.

After breakfast I gave Marrow the one job that I knew he would hate, yes you guessed, he had to clean out the latrines.

We had six in total and he had to clean them out and wash them using sea water.

He didn't like heights that much either, so the trek down and back up the cliff was quite a chore for him, but I never had any trouble from him for the rest of the tour so it did some good.

When we returned to our base in Devises we had quite a few stories to tell our families.

My family consisted of at that time, Gwen my wife and three children.

We flew back to Brize Norton and then onto the regimental lines in Devises.

After our return from Cyprus it was decided that we would be moving lock stock and barrel to Germany a place called Lippstadt, this as it turned out is just south east of Paderborn where I had been earlier in my career, which reminded me of the time that the regiment that I was then with 24 Regt had to share duties with the American soldiers.

The Regiment did its tour of duty guarding a warhead compound that belonged to the Americans.

We took this in turn with other Regiments, every one who took part in this tour were convinced, that we were only guarding the American Armies supply of Coke Machines, this idea came about as we had been informed that, out of the seven sites throughout Germany, only one housed the real nuclear warheads, and only the American top brass knew which site that was.

The nuclear war-heads were for use of the missile Regiments of the American and British Armies, in the event of a war with Russia breaking out. Thankfully it didn't, on one tour we had the company of the Ban the Bomb Brigade who just disrupted the coming and going of supplies for those soldiers guarding the site. This obviously didn't endear them to us at all but then that was not why they were there.

The more disruption that was caused the better, the disruption lasted the whole of one weekend, then as Sunday night set in the crowds started to leave in dribs and drabs until the outside of the compound was completely clear to our relief. Anyway back to the Regimental move.

We set up the Regiment this time I was not on the Advance Party but the change over was smooth.

We cleared everything then started to retrain all the lads on different guns as this was a posting to a completely mobile gun called a S.P. self propelled gun I remember being on one exercise when at the mid point the regiment had a drivers competition which consisted of a drive through woods being directed by your vehicle commander, then a drive through the woods on your own, followed by a night drive then a day drive battened down both the commanded drive and the battened down drive was done in a tracked vehicle.

Each driver had to drive three different vehicles to take part in the competition and from each Battery we had four drivers, I was one, Dave was the second, Bumpy was the third and Jock the fuel truck driver was the fourth from our Battery. In the first round Jock was knocked out, in the second round Bumpy and Dave were knocked out leaving me to go through in the last two rounds.

I got through and the last round was between me and a Sergeant, from another Battery. You have no chance of beating him said Bumpy, thanks I said you are a great help, you'll be ok Mick came a shout from Dave.

It turned out that we both scored the same points so we had to have a time trial round the course, which included going through trees and over some really rough terrain.

Still we scored the same points; I was eventually named the winner after it transpired that our friendly sergeant had cheated in the questions part of the competition, this event turned out to be an annual event and was a welcome relief for the lads during the long summer exercises.

Each trial was different from the one the previous year.

While we were on one of these summer exercises I had impressed enough to be picked to do some air ops, this was the first time that I had been given the chance to carry out this type of Observation post duty.

It required my taking part in an extra exercise but I didn't mind at all as it was a new experience for me.

I met the helicopter pilot whose name was Flight Sergeant Eusanne the spelling may not be correct but it was certainly French sounding and French spelling but he spoke perfect English.

He asked me had I been up before, no I replied, well you have nothing to worry about, I am told that you are the top o.p-ack at the moment, thank you I said, well lets go.

We took off and went round in circles for a while to allow me to get my bearings, the pilot helped by giving me some pointers when I was ready we started the fire mission.

During a fire mission radio operators have a certain procedure to follow so that the mission goes off without incident or accident and having finished a dry run mission I was given a live firing mission of six guns with a total of six rounds per gun, if required, however the mission is nearly always cut short for o.p-acks so as to save ammunition.

I started the mission and at a pre determined point in the mission the Helicopter drops down out of the sky rapidly, as we are on the flight path of the shell, so that we do not get shot out of the sky, we are then warned, by the gun post signaller by the phrase "splash over" so that we can come up and observe the shell landing. There we were up in the air waiting for the operator to say shot and time of flight, but we received the words "splash over" instead, this means that the round has passed us or really close to us.

The pilot just cut his engine and we dropped out of the sky like a stone, my insides were still in the air and the pilot was swearing and cursing so much that even I blushed.

The radio operator had a mouth full of abuse the gun post officer got the same and when we landed again I thought that he was going to kill some one he went berserk.

I was still shaking after we had been debriefed on our mission.

The outcome from this was that I was taken up again by the same pilot and we did further fire missions, to get it out of my system and to show that when performed correctly it works fine.

The radio operator was put onto driving only; the gun post officer was given a royal dressing down by the colonel and the Instructor in Gunnery who observes on most exercises, I just got more experience of flying with the Army Air Corps, but will never forget that experience ever.

After we returned to camp we set to cleaning and servicing the vehicles for the Annual Unit Equipment Inspection normally called the UEI.

The time arrived for us to embark to Canada, I was lucky to be on the advance party, at the time I thought Jesus why me this is just what I didn't want but I had to put up with it.

We travelled by BAC111 to Canada, we had been flying for about two hour's before we were given our first meal on board, we reached the far out post of Gand airstrip after a six hours flight, the plane landed at Gand we had to alight so that ground crew could refuel the aircraft for the last part of our journey. This was the longest stint of the whole flight, although we had arrived in Canada we still had Eight hours flight time.

I remember saying to myself why the hell does it take so long to travel over land when it didn't take that long over the ocean, stupid I said stupid idiot, muttering to myself. The distance from Gand to Calgary is greater than that of England to Gand.

We arrived in Calgary very tired and flight weary but this did not make any difference to the BSM who as soon as we landed started to shout and yell at every one to move out onto the tarmac and line up in three ranks. Out we all fell tripped or stumbled, you look like a lot of down and outs shouted the BSM for crying out loud get yourselves sorted out now.

We all shuffled about, then lined up, dressed off and waited for are orders, by the right quick march, and off we marched to the Terminal to retrieve our baggage, then through customs and onto our Coaches. These were new fresh and cool and each seat was a recliner, we set off and told that in an hour or so we would be stopping for food. Christ al mighty how far have we got to travel mate I asked the driver only two hundred miles he said not far.

Off we set I don't think that any body saw any of the trip to the halfway stage as we all slept. At the halfway stop the restaurant was called, yes very corny "The Halfway House" I sat at a table, which had a spare seat and waited to be served. The waitress who seemed to have legs up to her armpits and a very short skirt asked if I wanted anything to eat, yes please I'll have a beef burger and fries, ok sir would you like the burger loaded or standard, what! Quick as a flash I said, I want eat the bloody thing not shoot it; she then went on to explain what she meant.

A standard burger was a half pound beef burger in a large bun with lettuce tomato and dill pickle served with fries.

A loaded burger was the same as the standard with the same again on top with two eggs in the middle of each layer, this made it a four decked burger and you needed to be very hungry to be able to eat you way through such a large feast. But soldiers being what they are some of them managed to eat a loaded burger with double fries.

It wasn't long before we started the last leg of the trip, most of us by this time had slept all we needed to and just wandered at the sights. The vast size of open spaces the Alberta Prairies were huge and at various points along the way we could see the settlements of the Black foot tribes.

We could not tell from our transport if a settlement was Indian tribesman or white Canadian, but the driver gave us a running commentary as to who was who. At times we would cross a rail track, and at one such crossing we had to wait for a train to pass. The train had four Engines one at the front two at different points in the middle and one at the rear it took all of twenty minutes for the train to go over the crossing I was beginning to think that it wasn't going to end it was so long.

We proceeded on our way and with all the different things to see and wander at we soon arrived at the Camp, the name of our home for the coming training season was called, Camp Crowfoot. The Camp was about three miles from the nearest town this was called Medicine Hat and was on the edge of the Alberta Prairie's.

After unloading our cases and kit bags from the coach we were ushered into the camp Mess hall for a briefing of our duties for the next week until the main part of the Regiments joined us.

As this was a Battle Group Training period we had the pleasure as the RSM put it of training with the Royal Tank Regiment and the Royal Irish Rangers.

Our observers were from the royal Canadian Artillery and the Canadian Infantry and were made up of two Majors, these were

Instructors in Gunnery and three Captains who were trained in the art of Battle Group tactics.

We would be monitored from the day we drove out of the camp until the evening we drove back to the Regimental lines (camp). We also learned that we would also be directed from time to time as to the outcome of our Battles so that we could also monitor our progress throughout the training.

The one piece of information that was greeted with glee from every soldier from Gunner to Officer was that while serving at Crowfoot we would not be required to perform any duties, as these were undertaken by Canadian Civilian employees. After the meeting a couple of us lads went into town for a couple of drinks we found a pub and entered, Canadians call they pubs, Taverns, we ordered our drinks and made another mistake.

I asked for three beers please, we were told to sit at any table and the drinks would be carried to us, we sat and within seconds of sitting down the drinks were plonked on the table we all looked at each other.

What the hell is that said Dave, three beers said the waitress, but we only wanted three pints said bumpy, well in Canada that means three Jugs of beer, we didn't argue we just drank, in each jug there was three glasses of beer and we ordered another round.

After a while we all decided to have something to eat so Dave asked if a restaurant was close, yes said the barman but we can serve you food, what would you like?

Do you have a menu? Yes he said and gave us one each, we all ordered two rounds of Ham sandwiches, Mistake number three, are you sure you want two rounds each? he asked so I said why? Well we have three whole sandwiches in one round, so we all changed the order to just two rounds between us.

When we received the food our eyes popped out, Jesus I said I am really glad that we changed the order, the Bread was lovely and fresh but rather thick cut and the Ham was just as thickly cut.

Only bumpy managed to eat all of his, Dave and I concentrated on the beer. We chatted to a couple of the locals, who advised us as to the best places in town and the best places to avoid made more idle chat before returning to camp by Taxi.

51

The Regiment arrived on time and all the vehicles were inspected and signed for by the drivers and equipped with our own kit and ready to roll within two days of the other Regiments arriving.

The day came for us to start our first Battle Group Training session; this was really funny as the only members of the regiments that had been out on the prairies were those who came over on the advance party.

Being on the prairie was like being in the dessert not too many land marks to go by, we had vehicles getting lost all over the place, at that time the best way to navigate was to.

A. use the Telegraph poles which ran from north to south, or due to the fact that Suffield had been used for Nuclear Tests some years back and graders had cut out wide and fairly deep furrows at different distances from the epicentre.

I, E, one at three miles then at five miles and again at seven miles, and then in two mile steps. So all you had to do was drive round one of the ruts and measure how far you had travelled then when you arrived at the Telegraph poles you could work out where you were. That was the theory anyway, but vehicles and drivers still got lost and were not seen again for a couple of days in one case but normally only hours.

Now what happened on the first weeks exercise, we tried to become accustomed to the heat, no chance what so ever, it was bloody hot and each time we stopped every vehicle was inundated with flies, millions of the damn things.

We leagued up at night my vehicle being in the middle of a ring of Chieftain Tanks, as I was in the OP vehicle for the gunners, who were ten to fifteen miles away. I was the liaison for our guns to give support to the infantry and the tanks if and when required. The first morning my radio operator cooked breakfast, he gave the OP officer and me our cup of tea while he cooked, then he served us with our breakfast just as he did the wind started to blow rather hard.

My plate was covered in sand and it was every where in the cup of tea in the breakfast, completely ruined. I tried to eat some but I couldn't so I left it, my officer ate his, but within minutes he was throwing it all back up again, serves him right said geordie, the greedy git.

To keep the water cool we were issued with a bag made of cow hide, which we had to soak before filling with water and the said bag had to be covered in mud to stop it leaking, and this did work.

The water stayed cool for the whole day even though the sun shown down on it. Day seven halfway through the first exercise we had a Sunday sermon from the Regimental Padre. We all sat in a large culvert with three sides and an open end, the lads sat on one side of the culvert while the Padre stood and preached from the opposite side.

Halfway through the service three late arrivals strolled over the hill behind the Padre this was met by every one even the colonel cracking up with laughter. It just seemed so funny at the time due to the fact the Padre had started the service by reminding all that he felt like he was giving the sermon on the mount.

I don't think the Padre lived that down for months poor chap, still serves him right if you ask me.

On the day we were returning to camp, after completing the first exercise I was asked to drive a two and half tonne vehicle and get the Padre back as soon as possible as he had to go back to Calgary for a plane to Edmonton.

Off we set and took a short cut across country, the truck bumped and jumped all over the place and each time we bumped the Padre would put his hands on a box that he had stowed under his seat.

We hit one really big rut and the truck bounced up and down so hard that this box flew out from under the seat and burst open and the contents just emptied out inside the cab of the truck.

I looked down in horror, Jesus Padre what the f--- are you doing with them, as I said this I leapt out of the door and left the Padre to his devises, bloody idiot I thought as I picked myself up off the ground and brushed myself down, he must be bloody mad.

The vehicle came to a halt about fifty yards from me I gingerly walked up to the truck and shouted are you alright Padre? Yes no thanks to you, you silly man he replied, me silly I said you're the one who is carrying live Rattle snakes you must be mad I said.

He laughed and said don't worry bombardier I have milked them and all of them are safe. As I looked into the cab I could see that he had the box closed again.

Are you sure that you have them all I said, sure he replied, I will not say anything about your behaviour he said, I was scared of them once but I soon got used to them, not me I said I hate the things there make my skin crawl.

We reached the camp and I said goodbye to the Padre, glad to see the back of him for a while. The rest of the vehicles returned about four hours after I had and I was just waiting for the lads so we could go out for a drink.

After all the vehicles had been cleaned and stowed away we decided to hit the town. This time it was Dave, Graham and me off went into town, after a couple of drinks in the tavern, Dave went back to camp.

Graham and I went onto the dance hall in the town centre we chatted to a couple of girls, and I became real friendly with one and asked her name, Roseanne came the reply, well Roseanne can I walk you home after the dance? Sorry she said but it's too far to walk, came the answer, well ok then, we can go by bus I said, sorry came the reply, no busses go that way at this time of night.

Well how about we take a taxi I asked, well that would be rather expensive she said. You really don't want me to take you home then I said, it would be nice Roseanne replied, then what's wrong.

Well I live quite a way out, how far I said, two hundred miles she replied, in Calgary, What! I stammered two hundred miles, Christ no wander she said it would be expensive by taxi.

I felt such a nerd, I must have gone bright red, don't worry my dad is picking me up later but can I see you again she said, and we arranged to meet the following weekend at the camp.

Not much happened that week apart from me thinking that Roseanne would not turn up but she did and I was introduced to her dad and brother who was being dropped at a friends house for the week end.

We returned to Calgary and I met the rest of the Family, Mum Gyp the dog and two Siamese cats called Gert and Daisy, "I don't know why, don't ask me" came the reply when I asked, why Gert and Daisy. Roseanne's dad took us into the City and we had a great time we visited the Post Office tower replica of the one in London.

I was treated to dinner at a posh Bistro after which, we went to a Tavern and had a couple of beers before going back to the house.

The weekend passed so quickly that I didn't really enjoy it as much as I would have liked to but what the hell it turned out to be a free week end so who's complaining.

After that week end I didn't see Roseanne again we just didn't get in touch with each other although we changed addresses I still haven't heard from her, to this day.

I guess she will be married with 2.4 kids by now, but the memory of her still lingers from time to time.

She was quite a beautiful girl same height as me with a nice figure and most of all she had a great sense of humour, and long dark brown hair with blue/green eyes. Oh well c'est la vie.

We were called up on parade on the Monday morning for a shock report.

The RSM was looking rather agitated, every one was whispering to each other, what is the matter? What's wrong? Right gentlemen shouted the Colonel as he started to address us I have some bad news, and it is that, last night one of the Irish Rangers was walking back to Camp when he was involved in a hit and run accident, unfortunately he has since died.

I would like those who, saw anything or has heard of anything to come forward to assist in the conviction of the person responsible, who is at this time under arrest in Calgary. So that you are all aware of what happened the local Police have asked me to pass on to you this message if any one can help please do so thank you. RSM you may dismiss the parade.

The parade fell out in silence we as gunners didn't know the lad who had been killed but we still felt upset as we had lost a comrade needlessly by a senseless drunk driver.

We prepared for the mornings training prior to our next exercise and at lunchtime we had yet more bad news.

It would seem that one of the Tankies had, whilst loading his tank with a H.E, shell caught his hand in the breech of the gun and had severed his hand off from the wrist, he was rushed to the nearest hospital but their were unable to save his hand. Poor bugger said Andy at the lunch table, some one said that he, "the lad who lost his hand" was thinking of the lad who got killed last night, said Graham.

How do you know that said Bumpy, well the Irish lad was his mate and he was out drinking with him but decided to come back to camp early, and now he is blaming himself. Poor bugger said Andy, cant you say anything else other than that I said, oh piss off mike you know me, man of few words, man of piss all I said, Andy got up in a huff and left.

After the second exercise was over we had a couple of days up in the Banff National park, I travelled up in a land-rover with the BC and Graham, I drove the second leg from Calgary to Banff Graham had driven the first leg from the Camp to Calgary, with me showing the way which wasn't too hard as it was a straight road from Medicine Hat and the road was equally as straight on the second leg.

When we reached Banff the BC took the Land Rover onto Lake Jasper while Graham and I stayed in Banff under canvas by the side of Lake Louise.

We decided that we did the right thing by not going to Jasper with the BC. Lake Louise is the most beautiful spot in the Rocky Mountains within the Alberta Province, it was quiet the Lake was fresh the Bow River ran into and out of the area to the east of the Lake and was brimming with fish and the sight and sounds of the whole area was fantastic.

We felt that yes we did stay in the better area; we had plenty of bars to choose from for beer at night and loads of sights to see during the day.

We rode on horseback up to the ice fields, we bathed in the hot sulphur springs, we visited the old fort, which was the Mounties Head Quarters and we rode on the cable car up the side of the mountain. We saw salmon leaping in the Bow river, we even saw Grisly Bears. When Rest and Recuperation was over and the Major returned to pick us up to return to the camp we had loads of tales to tell him.

But he was not very amused when we told him that we had seen a Bear up real close. What do you mean up close bombardier he said, well sir! I replied we were sleeping in the car that we had hired, due to having to much beer that night we decided to sleep in a lay by. At about three in the morning, Bombardier "T" woke me telling me to look out the window, this I did and all I could see was this bloody great big brown Bear.

Well! Said the BC what happened then? I was just getting to that I replied, the car was being shaken, by this Bear and we were terrified.

Then we heard a loud hailer from a helicopter telling the occupants of the car to drive off but slowly until we had got away from the Bear, so I fought my way out of my sleeping bag and started the car and drove away from the Bear slowly, as I did so the Bear scratched the top of the car with both sets of claws when I was clear I just sped off like a dart until I was stopped by the chopper landing on the road in front of us.

A Mountie got out and gave us the biggest rocket we have ever received, but we had deserved it as we had been told not to stop on the road because of the Bears.

We thanked our luck that we had got away with a ticking off as well as just a scratch on the car.

On hearing this the BC said, well I never, I spent all that time at Jasper with my camera, just to get a photo of a Bear and didn't see one only to hear that, you nearly get killed by one.

I think he had the sulks for a couple of days, still I suppose I would have been upset if the situation had been reversed.

The rest of the time that we spent at Suffield went by without further incident, photographs of gophers, snakes and lads with they vehicles and in or out side tents, with groups or on there own.

We had a final exercise and were lucky to see the most beautiful Aurora Borealis "The Northern Lights" the spectacle was amazing as the different colours danced across the skies for which seemed like ages, this was immediately followed by the most horrendous storm which had been travelling toward us all day when it struck it must have been about midnight, we all laid under the tents which were not pitched as we were told not too but just to lay under them until the rain stopped.

What we didn't know at that time was that we would be joined by other animals like rattle snakes and bugs and other such creepy crawlies, which we got rid off pretty damn quick when the rain did stop.

After the training was complete we returned to Germany and Lippstadt Ackassienne, Strasse, number 24, Lippstadt, this was where I lived when not on exercise or duty Gwen my wife and the children shared a flat just beside the main railway line from the south Muenchen Gladbach to the north and places like Hannover, Minden and other towns.

The force's families complained to the local town council that due to the line not having a fence on either side of it, so therefore the line was a danger to the children. The answer we received was not one that we expected.

The town councillors decided that we English families must teach our children not to go near the lines, as none of the German children do and had never had an accident involving children in the towns history so we should not complain. That was the end of that.

I remember one weekend it was decided that we would hold a party in the cellar of one of the buildings, which was quite large "the cellar that is." We invited most of the families baby-sitters and some friends too, we all clubbed together so that we could buy the beer and food.

Most of the wives cooked the food and made quite a good spread of goodies, we started at seven in the evening. The music was low to start with, but as the night passed then the music became louder and louder, to the point when we received a visit from the local Politzie informing us that Germans, do not make such noises and we must stop the noise. So as not to disturb our German neighbours, we turned the music down enough for us to dance too.

After the police had gone one lad got upset and was going to take on the whole of the Germans in the town, we restrained him, calmed him down and then he fell asleep so we left him to sleep, so we thought, this wasn't his intention at all.

While we were still enjoying the music and drinking the lad decided that he was going to teach the Germans a lesson. He was in the street with his trousers round his ankles mooning to the houses where the Germans lived and shouting for them to "come and kiss my arse" and "we beat you once and we can do it again".

We dragged him back to the flats and calmed him down, hoping that nobody had seen him, Reg said that he had enough beer and he would stay with the lad, to ensure he didn't get into any trouble, the rest of us returned to the party. Partying was one way for us to let off some steam, but we had to be careful that we didn't upset the local community.

I think that most of the families got on well with them; it seemed that the single lads of the Regiment had most trouble trying to get to know them. This may have been due to the amount of single mothers who had dated English lads in the past and had become pregnant; the lads had then been posted and not heard of again by the girls.

This wasn't good relations at all, but I think that most German towns where English soldiers were had the same or similar problem.

Well it was now time for me to be demobilised as I had served Nine years and at that time I felt that it was time for me to join the ranks of civilians. I had been to England on leave to find employment which I did, I was going to start with the Post Office Telephone's as a trainee, telephone engineer, at Jerome Street, in London, just behind Spitalfields Fruit Market.

Before leaving Germany I was given an inscribed Tankard. From the NCO'S Mess and demob party, by the lads in the Battery bar. I was really sorry to be leaving them, but at the time, it was the right thing to do.

As I was talking to one of the Officers during the evening of the party he said that I would be back within six months so we had a five pound bet. He went on to ask me why the men thought he was a twit, and didn't respect him. "Are you sure you want me to answer" that I asked. "Yes" came his reply. "Ok, well, it's like this, I started.

When you first came to the Battery, you had an air of superiority that rubbed the lads up the wrong way, in that, you had just come from Officer training school [Sandhurst] you have to remember, these lads had been in the Regiment longer than you had served to date. Your attitude towards them was one of, {I know better}, but you don't! Reading books doesn't give you the knowledge the gun crews have, plus most of the gun crews, where doing live firings while you were still at sixth form school.

With lots of experiences behind them on different type guns, then along comes a young Sub/Lieutenant and tries to tell them their job, in a manner befitting an arsehole, so you asked for all the trouble that you got. So if you want to win the lads back the first thing to do is, become one of them, roll up your sleeves and get yourself dirty with them, listen to them speak with them not at them.

It will take a lot of that sort of work to win them over, let them see that you are willing to get stuck in and you will be the winner." He looked at me and said. "Would you have told me that if you had not been leaving?" "Yes I would, if you had asked," I replied. "Well in that case I will try to do as you have suggested and see how things go."

"Don't forget to give it a good trial period, it will not happen over night, you have a lot of bridges to mend," with that he thanked me for being frank with him, then he bought every one in the bar a drink. Bumpy asked me what I had said to him, "just a few home truths Bumpy, that's all."

"Well I hope he gets the message or he is going to get decked and I am not the only one who wants to deck him." I told bumpy that I knew and that I didn't think that any one would have any trouble with him from now on.

I bid my farewell to the lads and left the party, so that I could get ready for my departure the following morning. The time arrived that I was to leave all the mates that I had made over the years, I was sad but at the same time glad that I was leaving. At that time, I thought that, by no means, would I be going back, and wandered how I was going to get my winnings from the bet that I had taken up with the officer.

I didn't dwell on it too much though, I was more interested in the thought of being a civilian and working for the GPO as a Telephone Engineer, and looking forward to not getting up before sparrows fart each morning and not being screamed at by BSM's or drill Sergeants.

I didn't at that time know why, but I would find myself back in uniform again serving with the same lads that I had just left behind in Germany. It's a funny old world, don't you think?

CHAPTER 5

Having left the Army I started work at the Post Office Telephones as it then was, it is now British Telecom, I worked from Jerome Street, which was at the back of Spitalfields Fruit Market, each morning having got off the train at Liverpool Street Station, I would walk through Spitalfields, only to be met by quite a few down and out men who would when it was cold be huddled round a fire of old fruit boxes and any other wood which could be burnt just to keep them warm.

On one occasion as I walked through two guys started to fight and where going at each other like a couple of kids, slapping each others faces and shouting and of course swearing at each other too, until the police pulled in and all of them ran off except one man who was still sat by the dying fire when the police walked over to him he just keeled over, whether he was drunk I didn't know but found out through the local stall holders that he had died of consumption.

Anyway as I said I worked out of Jerome Street which was Tower Hamlets Exchange at that time or one of them, during my training I was paired with a man could Tom Smith, a likely name I know but it's true, Tom was and old chap in his early sixties and walked every where with his tool bag and safety guard over his shoulder and constantly had a cigarette between his lips even when he spoke that fag stayed put until he had smoked every last strand of tobacco from it, then he would just spit it out and roll another and stick it in it's place.

He would turn up just after me and we would ask the area engineer what jobs we had for the day and we would leave, we used to get about eight jobs each day some times we would complete them all

61

sometimes not, we then walked to the café just off Spitalfields church I think it was called St Martins in the Field.

We would chat to the other engineers before starting our day at around 10.30 ish, because we were situated in a rather built up area, as I said earlier we walked every where, on the odd occasion we would visit a Jewish tailor shop and would always be able to obtain some really good hand made shirts at a fraction of the normal price.

On one occasion we had to visit an address and Tom was not happy about it as he had tried on several occasions to gain entry to the property only to be told that he couldn't, however this day we had managed to gain entry but it was one of those days when I wish I had stayed at home, as we walked in it had a very noticeable smell, in fact the place stank of really strong body odour, in each room down stairs and upstairs bodies were sleeping we had to step over the sleeping people to get at the phones, this job was to resituate the main phone a simple job but it took about three quarters of an hour to complete, boy were we glad to get out of that house.

On another occasion we were sat at a footway junction box fixing some local telephone cables under an umbrella as it was thrashing down with rain both of us getting wet when Tom told me to take these two wires, I grabbed them, as I had tested wires out in the training and felt that fifty volts was not strong, however what I didn't know "but Tom did" was that it was what at that time was called a ringer.

It wasn't a telephone line but a fax line and was being used at the time we cut it off, I was holding the receiving end of the line, and as I was wet I got a bigger jolt than expected where upon I dropped the line, to the joy of Tom who just curled up laughing at my misfortune, I believe I might have swore at him something about his parentage or lack off, and yes when we returned to the exchange later that day I was the butt of the jokes.

I served about nine months in London and got quite fed up of the rude people who would brush past you while trying to fix telephone lines, everyone was in a hurry and had to get to where ever they were going yesterday so I asked for a transfer out of London to Enfield but only Watford, was available so I agreed to the transfer but the area engineer was willing to change my request if I wanted to return to London at any time, which I thanked him for.

On my arrival at the Watford depot. I worked out of Junction Road depot, which as the name implies, was at the rear of Watford Junction train station, but the exchange was in exchange road in the middle of Watford town just round the corner from Vicarage Road, Watford's football ground.

I was paired up with a chap called Ron Parrot who was a real funny lad we were about the same age range give or take a couple of years, me being slightly older, after working with Ron for a while I was allowed out on my own with my own van but we still worked together most of the time.

Eric Tripp was our area engineer and after a while I was put in for upgrading, this caused a storm of protests from a couple of chaps that where the same grade as I was, but I was the only one to be proposed for up grading, an objection was made by a union rep for the other chaps but was turned down, the union thought that as I had been at Watford for less time than the other chaps I should be the last to be upgraded.

The issue was resolved quite quickly as it was suggested by the union that we all work with a union rep for two weeks to see if we came up to the level required for upgrade, I was assured that I had nothing to worry about just do the job as I was trained to do with emphasis on the "by the book" I read the rules book over a couple of days the asked Ron if someone was taking the mickie, but he said no and that if a work to rule was every called for this was the way we did the job, so I did just that, I worked by the book.

Each day the union rep would secure my jobs and off we would go, while I carried out my work the rep would ask me different questions as to why I was doing things in the way that I was, could I have done it differently, my answers where always straight to the point, I also made sure that each time I had to open a footway box I would clean it out first before starting any repair.

When going to any cabinet I would ensure that all PO Telephone protocol was followed, I think that this got up the nose of the Union rep because he started to just sit in the van by the end of the first week, he said he had seen enough, and would speak to Mr Tripp on the following monday.

That weekend was a bit nerve raking but I needn't have worried as I was told on the Monday I had gained my upgrade, so more money great, also from then I was able to go out on protracted duty which meant that if you worked overtime past midnight any hours you worked the following day was paid at double time but you could only do this three times a week, I think if you tried more you would burn out anyway.

It wasn't long before I was missing the guys from the Regiment although I didn't pine for them, I didn't feel that civilian life was affording me as much camaraderie and I think that this was what I missed more than anything else, yes I had friends, but it just wasn't the same, so one day when I had heard from one of the lads that the Regiment was going to Northern Ireland I decided to sign on again.

I did talk this over with my wife and family first, we all agreed that I should just do it, so on 06 July 1970 I duly re-enlisted in her Majesties Forces "another shilling" another nine years.

CHAPTER 6

Back in the Cake

I reported to Woolwich Garrison on the 10th of July 1970 and was kitted out and just had to have a medical to ensure that I was still fit enough to be swore at, shouted at and even as it turned out shot at, and of course I was.

Two days later I was given my orders for rejoining the 27th Med Regiment RA my flight out was on the 16th July I was taken to Gatwick Airport and flew to RAF Gutersloh in Western Germany along with families travelling back from blighty leave and even some Kids joining families from Boarding schools.

The flight was fairly uneventful, I arrived at Gutersloh to be met by the PRI bus that always picked up soldiers returning from leave and new intake squaddies from training, at that time the bus was driven by German civilians and were always helpful with heavy cases that some kiddies had.

On my return to the Regiment I was greeted by the RSM at the guardroom who told me that I had to report to the HQ where I would be told which Battery I was going to, although I already knew I still thought it a good idea to do as I was told, when I reached the office I was asked why was I reporting to them and not to the battery office, so I shuffled off to the Battery lines.

I reached the Battery and went straight to the store for some bedding. "Hello mate, came the voice from jock the store man, what can I do for you," he asked. "Some bedding please jock." I answered "Ok Bomb," he said. "Whoa I am only a gunner Jock," I said. "Sorry mate, he said I forgot last time you were here we drank together in the mess." "Not anymore mate well at least not yet."

"You have to report to the office as the Billy Wills wants to see you." "Ok jock thanks for that." I took my bedding to the room which I was to use for a while and went down to the Battery office, as I entered I was met by the young officer that I had been speaking to before I left who said that I would be back within six months. "Well I guess I got that wrong then Bomb." he said, "Sorry sir I am only a gunner now." "Well I suppose I owe you a fiver then, he said. "I guess you do sir" I answered and he went out the building muttering something about not being wrong just at the length of time.

Billy Wills called me into his office when he saw me talking to then Battery clerk, I entered and came to attention in front of his desk. "Ok stand easy young man, well it's nice to see you back but I have bad news for you and that is, you will have to start from the bottom again, as I have other soldiers that have been here for some time that would take exception to you getting promoted as soon as you get back, do you understand." "Yes sir I do, I wasn't expecting to be promoted straight away or even at all sir." "Good glad we got that sorted out he said, keep you nose clean and you will be ok I have put you with Sergeant Bass as his second in command for the Ulster trip, so report to him as soon as you are sorted in your billet."

I joined Alfie in the garage area we had a chat and he asked when I would be promoted, my answer was simple I don't know haven't got a clue.

I wish I had a pound for every time that was Asked I would be worth a few quid now, well I didn't have long to wait to go to Ulster we flew out two weeks after I rejoined the Regiment.

We had some hairy moments while there we first went to a place called "Long Kesh" which was an old disused Airfield which was to become a prison for the IRA, UVF, UDF and others so with the Royal Engineers we started to build a perimeter fence all round the whole airfield while we were doing this other engineers were building H blocks for the prisoners who at this time were being kept prisoner on HMS Belfast in Belfast Docks, "Long Kesh" would become renamed "The Maze Prison" with the H Blocks becoming rather well known.

We also did patrols of the villages in and around the area from Bally Kinlar to Belfast and from Bangor to London Derry and all points in between, on some occasions we had to do searches of vehicles in road blocks most local people were good and took it all in their stride but we often had problems with profanities being directed at us, even when we patrolled the towns and villages we were subjected to the most foul mouthed taunts from adults male and female even by very young children, this would upset most of the guys as most of us had kids of our own and to hear these kids say the things that were being said was one hell of a wrench.

We had to go into all sorts of situations that were completely alien to all of us telling staff in telephone exchanges that we had been told that a bomb had been left in the building and everyone was to get out so that we could find it and either diffuse it or blow it up, but the Girls would just tell us "Oh Piss off there's no bomb here." But wouldn't leave, at any cost.

We did Border patrols day and night we even got ourselves a name that followed us around but it was out of respect for the way we went about our business, calm quick fair and without prejudice, but when ever we were about things would go quiet,

All the time we were in Ulster I was still being asked when I would be getting promoted, Billy Wills said to me one day "What's going on young man people keep asking me when you are being promoted." "Don't ask me, I answered, I keep getting the same question and all I can say to them is I don't know." "Well let me tell you, as far as I am concerned you won't be getting promoted in the near future if at all is that clear." "Yes sir" I said.

That evening as we were having our allowance of one beer Alfie asked if anything was wrong, "No not really I was wondering how I had upset Billy Wills." "Why" he asked. "Well he told me earlier that I will not be getting promoted in the near future if at all, and I haven't even asked to be promoted." "I keep being asked as well" said Alfie. "Well now you know what I know so perhaps you can tell everyone the same, that I am not getting promoted."

"I will" he said and we drank up and went of to our respective beds.

We finished our first tour of Northern Ireland with less casualties than expected two lads died when a bomb was thrown into the Sanger there were in, one lad was shot in the head but was ok no brain damage at all and Bumpy got shot in the wrist and the bullet missed all his bones and tendons lucky bugger but he still got to go back to the Regimental Lines in Germany early, the funny thing was that he was more upset at the thought of losing his tobacco, as he was rolling a cigarette at the time he was shot and the tin of baccy flew out of his hand up in the air and scattered everywhere he lost the lot.

On our return to Germany we had a party, well actually several parties.

About three months after we returned from Ireland I was called into Billy Wills office, I thought here we go again more pet talks about not getting promoted, I knocked on his door and was told to enter. "Ah Hook I have some good news for you, you are to be promoted to Lance Bombadier as of tomorrow, now as far as I am concerned we have men in this Battery that should be promoted before you, so make sure that you do a damn good job or you will be down faster than you can blink." "Yes sir thank you sir," I answered. "Now go to the store and get your stripes and make sure you have then in the morning."

The following morning everyone was congratulating me on my promotion, Alfie Bass came up to me saying, "I thought you wasn't getting promoted Mick, you said in Ireland." "I know I interrupted, I told you what I had been told so I am as shocked as you are."

We did the normal exercise on Hohne Ranges, Bisbingen cross roads and such places until we were told that we would be going back to Ireland for another tour, but this time we would get some training on urban warfare by the SAS.

I did several courses passed them all became an instructor for driving and maintenance on all types of wheeled and track laying vehicles, became a First Aid lay instructor and did a Gun Survey course passed that and ended up getting promoted again to Bombadier took up being the BKs OP ack the BK was Captain Ian Dury, later to become Brigadier.

The BC was Major (Snorkel) (Smith) and his OP ack was Bombadier Terry St Pierre we had quite a few laughs at his expense too, I recall being on exercise one time in Hohne and we had a weekend pass to go back to the families in Lippstadt this was only for the married soldiers "a little unfair but the single lads didn't much care, anyway we were all fed up of the BC scrounging food off us all at various times, so Terry decided to make him a rhubarb tart of his own after finding out that he enjoyed the last one Terry bought with him at the start of the exercise.

Terry, myself, Brian Smart, Graham Tune and numerous others went home for the week end on our return we all bought something to eat IE home made goodies Terry had two rhubarb tarts, he told us all that under no circumstance should we touch the one with the extra cross of pastry on top as this was for the BC, why we asked. "You brown nose git" I said.

"No you fool it's full of Sennacot to make him stop asking for food."

Well it wasn't long into the second day when his nibs decided that the tart we were eating looked rather nice. "Could one have a taste bombardier St Pierre?" "Yes of course sir" he said, so he went to the trailer and cut a piece from the one with Sennacot in handing it to the Major he said. "Enjoy sir, my wife made that." The only thing was, he accepted it, and went to his bivvy. "Wait for it said Terry that is full, he should crap through the eye of a needle when he has eaten it."

It must have been half hour after, when the BC came back for more, "Are you sure you should, asked Terry, after all it is rhubarb and is known to be a laxative."

"Oh that's fine," said the BC, so Terry cut him an even bigger piece this time and off the BC trundled again.

Well, that night we thought that we would all be awakened by the BC trying to scramble to the nearest latrine that had been dug, but no movement at all.

At breakfast we were just starting to do the eggs when out pops Snorkel "morning chaps I trust you all had a good nights rest? We have a heavy day in front of us so after breakfast we will be off, by the way bomb St Pierre that tart was rather nice, I don't suppose you have anymore do you?" "As it happens sir, I have on piece left."

"Oh well in that case I better not."

"No, that's ok sir, you have it, I think we all had enough thank you, so you are welcome to it."

When he had disappeared with the last slice of tart we all looked at each other in astonishment. "How the hell has he not had a crap yet," said Brian. "Christ! Said Terry, he has eaten enough to make a horse shite himself, let alone a human." "He's not normal," Said his driver Geordie. "You got that right, I said, he must have the constitution of an elephant." We finished of the breakfast, packed everything away and loaded the trailers, then waited for Snorkel to join us we had already been briefed on the day's activities.

Snorkel finally joined us and off we went as we drove over the ranges the BC and his crew went one way we, the BKs crew, went off in a different direction altogether, we carried out our duties for the next three days without seeing the BC and his crew.

However when we did meet up we asked how things went, it seems that the Major became rather unwell about tea time that day, after he had drunk a mug of tea he took off across the ranges with a shovel not to be seen for at least twenty minutes when he returned he was rather red round the gills, he asked for a cold drink of water and within a couple of minutes he was off again.

It would seem that he was under the misguided assertion that it was the water in the small water bowser that was not pure, he hadn't twigged that it was the rhubarb tart, but we know different don't we.

Not long after that episode we were given orders that we were to return to Northern Ireland for a further tour, and that I would head my own team the list was printed on orders and I was shocked to see that I had all the people other NCOs where glad there didn't.

We had training by a member of the SAS on urban warfare although we had been out before the problems in Ulster had become worse and more sophisticated as time had moved on so had the tactics of the locals.

At each set of training weeks all teams were tested and my team came last each time and I know that I was being watched by BSM Billy Wills in my mind he was waiting for me to trip up so he could demote me, but on the last test before going to Ulster I told the team that we were the laughing stock of the Regiment and that I didn't much like that, so lets show them we are as good if not better than the rest, it worked as we came third in the final test.

I was really chuffed that we had done so well from being last each time to third was one hell of a jump which proved that the team had what it took to do the job all we had to do now, was prove it for real, my Team were, my second in command was L/Bdr Adrian Chant, plus we had the team of misfits as we were called by all and sundry, but we didn't let it get us down we were made of sterner stuff, we had Shady Lane, who was to eventually be posted to become the Brigadiers Driver, Archie, Bob Evans, who I threatened to shoot and my Radio operator and carrier, the general, a bit of a disaster area always seemed to get himself in sticky situations, Ozzy was a tall spindle of a bloke who we either called Ozzy or the nose due to the size of his hooter or snapper, which ever fitted at the time where the names came from I haven't a clue.

I remember one time we were out on patrol and we were being led by none other than Capt T... when we walked through fields and peat bogs then we came to a river, I sent one of the lads to have a look at the bridge to ensure that it was safe to cross, but T... had other ideas. "We can't use the bridge men it may be booby trapped." "No traps at all sir," came a reply from the ranks. "Well never mind that, we will cross the river here men."

"Are you sure sir," I asked. "Yes Bomb, no problem." "It's bloody November its bloody cold and we have at least another three hours before we will be back at camp to change clothes sir," I said.

"Look Bomb I will cross first, I wouldn't ask you all to do something I am not prepared to do." Off he strode into the river, now this man was about six foot eight inches tall, and Myself and Bob Evans were only five six so you see he had the advantage of at least 14 inches over us, as he waded into the middle of the river the water came halfway up his chest.

"You do realise that we have two short arses in this team sir," I shouted.

"Oh shut up and get across Bombadier." So in we went holding our rifles above us as we went Christ the water was cold and as I said deep in the middle I had to jump up and down as I made my way across telling Bob to do the same.

Once across and out at the other side we picked up the pace for moving just to keep warm I must admit that we soon became dry as the sun came out it got a little warmer but not much, but, by the time we had got back to the billet we all sighed a sigh of relief, "I hope we don't have him with us all the time." said shady once our Officer had left us after our debrief. "The man is a nutter Mick, I hope you are going to complain to some one about that," said Bob.

"I will certainly try, I said, I did mention it in the debrief and the S.I.B. bloke looked at me as if I was mad, so I will ensure the BC is told lads." "Good for you Bomb." Came the chorus.

On another occasion we were at the drill hall in Enniskillen and we had an evening off and as long as we were in threes we could go to the local hop, some did, but some of us went to the local pub called the White Star, we had a great night the locals were friendly didn't ask us any questions about who we were or why we were in the town, I think everyone knew why we were there anyway, we had a sing song to a man playing a fiddle and I played my harmonica and a couple of the guys sang along with the locals it was a great night but we had to get back to the drill hall by ten pm so we had to leave early, but we were invited to go back at the week end, we said that we would try and left.

After a couple of weeks we were to move over to the local boat club on the side of Lough Erne and a couple of days later we heard the pub had been blown up, because the English Soldiers used it, but no one got hurt, even though the pub was burnt to the ground by the IRA. It was while we were at the boat house that Bumpy got shot the skiving git.

We did a few other patrols and had some skirmishes especially on the border patrols one day we were shot at and a gun battle took place we were pinned down on one side of a small valley with the other side of the valley being the south we could see the smoke from the small arms fire coming from a line of trees on the south side of the border (we had no such cover) so these were our targets, however I think more cows were shot that day than IRA.

We returned fire on the orders, of make sure of your target men before returning fire, barked out by an Officer from the rear, we did as ordered and I know that I was not alone in feeling a little bit worried at this point, but I doubt anyone pondered for long.

We started to withdraw and on reaching the withdrawal area we needed, I checked the crew to find that we were missing one man who was supposed to have been our main cover when on the retreat, who was armed with a Bren gun and box of ammunition when I asked where he was nobody knew, I asked for a volunteer to go get him and was met with silence, so it was up to me I had to go back for the lad who had not pulled back with the rest of us, knowing that he had the Bren Gun I knew where he should be and sure enough the poor bugger had frozen to the spot but a few sharp words and threats of some swift kicks up the backside did the trick, and we managed to get back to the lines without being shot, a couple came close but not too close I think.

Before that episode, one lad kept tripping over as we withdrew, one half of the team would pull back so many yards and then give covering fire for the other half to pull back and so on, but as I said one lad kept tripping he got so frustrated that at one point he fell down threw his rifle forward and said. "If the bastard wants to shoot me he can."

He was about fifteen yards in front of me so I levelled my rifle at him and shouted.

"If you don't get your arse moving I will shoot you before the IRA have a chance." With that he jumped up grabbed his rifle and flew past me and never tripped again, in hind sight, I think that all that activity with the tripping over made me take my eye of the ball something that I shouldn't have done.

After we were all checked in at the troop lines my section jumped up in the back of a four ton truck to take us back to camp, as we started to drive off the lad with the Bren Gun turned to me and said, "I suppose you think that was funny don't you, I at once said no I didn't and that it could happen to anyone, but that we were the only ones to know, unless he did something similar later, however he didn't so all was well that day god was on both our sides.

At the end of the day after our debriefing he (the lad who kept tripping) asked me if I had one up the spout when I pointed my rifle at him, of course I did I said, but I didn't, but he didn't know that did he.

When we returned to Germany after that tour Shady who had promised to buy me a crate of beer if I ensured he survived the tour, did indeed keep up to his promise and bought round to my flat a crate of brew which we sank quite readily, and if you ask me, did I earn it, hell yes I did.

I know that there are many more things that I could write about but would probably upset too many people, some embarrassing times for me and others.

So I will spare them and me the blushes, for now.

I would however like to mention that Big Ken George and myself did get a polite request from half the battery, while on one of our many exercise in Germany to keep quiet, as we had started to sing along round a fire one evening Ken playing his guitar me playing my Harmonica, with a couple of lads singing, sigh! Those were the days and I am sure that others had just as many if not more tales to tell.

* 1 Ac/Adj: - Assistant Adjutant.
* 2 OP/Ack: - Observation Post Officers Assistant.
* BC:- Battery Commander.
* BK:- Battery Captain.

I would like to thank some people for making life bearable and some guidance from time to time and companionship. I would also like to apologise for some of the stories being slightly altered so that no one would be embarrassed and for getting some names wrong with some of the incidents.

23 Medium Batt /27 Med Medium Regt. R.A.

Dave & Linn Trythall.	Ozzy the Nose.		
Paddy Swayne.	Ken George.		
Graham Tune.	Terry St Perrie		
Jeff Murray	Reg & Lynn Crouch,		
Clippie Higgs	Bob Evans		
Marrow Dochrey.	Paul (Shady) Lane	BSM Morgan	Archie Leslie
Bumpy Holmes.	Stanley Flinn		
BSM Billy Wills.	Adrian Chant	BSM Tony Gaunt.	Paddy McNair
Lieutenant Tressedar.	Captain Ian Dury		

Bombadier   2nd Lt. Entwhistle
Clements.

Bombadier B   Gunner Moody
Bethel.

And many many more who I haven't named

Royal Artillery School Larkhill
Missile Wing
Salisbury Plain Wiltshire

Scouser (wrecker driver).

Geordie Maggie.   Scottish Pat

L/Bdr Dibble.   Sgt Smith.

Capt Tommy Smith T.I.G.

51 Missile Battery 24 Missile Regt. R. A.
Nienburg Wesser and Paderborne
West Germany.

Des & Maureen Goldsworthy.   Andy Brown.

Pete (Pop) & Silvia Drybourgh.   Ginge Rowny. Chris & Christine Ainsworth

Major Evans.   Major Forsythe

Major Smith.   Johnny Gooding

2nd Lt I. Entwhistle. Major Smith

2nd Lt P Crump

24 *The Irish Training Battery. R.A. Oswestry Shropshire UK*

Johnny Cheeseman.

Plus many, many, more that I served with in different theatres and Regiments.

For the eighteen years that I served I had laughs and shared sad times, to those I may have forgotten in this book, I will hopefully put you in any further book I may write.

At this point I would like to thank my lovely wife for her support while trying to get this book together, without her support it would have been even more difficult than it was.

Lightning Source UK Ltd.
Milton Keynes UK
UKOW04f0026211115

263138UK00004B/51/P

The Ramblings of a Squaddie

to Nicola

Best Wishes

Michael Seaton

WARNING
THIS BOOK CONTAINS
STRONG LANGUAGE.
NOT SUITABLE FOR
CHILDREN

Copyright © 2015 by Michael Seaton.

ISBN: Softcover   978-1-5144-6155-6
               eBook   978-1-5144-6154-9

All rights reserved. No part of this book may be reproduced or transmitted in
any form or by any means, electronic or mechanical, including photocopying,
recording, or by any information storage and retrieval system, without permission
in writing from the copyright owner.

Any people depicted in stock imagery provided by Thinkstock are models, and
such images are being used for illustrative purposes only.
Certain stock imagery © Thinkstock.

Print information available on the last page.

Rev. date: 07/10/2015

The Ramblings of a Squaddie

MICHAEL SEATON